M000310608

Blow the Lid Off!

RECLAIM YOUR STOLEN CREATIVITY, INCREASE YOUR INCOME, AND LET YOUR LIGHT SHINE!

ROBERT BELLE

Dedication

I dedicate this book to all those people who have called me crazy and weird because of my ideas. You allowed me to realize that I just didn't fit with the "norms," and in turn, this has led me to live an authentic, creative, and sometimes crazy life.

I also dedicate this book to you, the reader. May you realize the creativity that is there inside you and waiting to come out so you can manifest your brilliance, your uniqueness, and your offerings to the world. You motivated me to write this book! Now let your light shine!

Copyright © 2019 Robert Belle

All rights reserved. No part of this publication may be reproduced, distributed, or transmitted in any form or by any means, including photocopying, recording, or other electronic or mechanical methods, without the prior written permission of the publisher, except in the case of brief quotations embodied in critical reviews and certain other noncommercial uses permitted by copyright law. For permission requests, write to the publisher, addressed "Attention: Permissions Coordinator," at the address below.

Contact information for Simply You Publishing- simplyyoupublishing@gmail.com

ISBN: 978-9966-136-14-5 (print)

ISBN: 978-996-136-15-2(ebook)

Ordering Information:

Special discounts are available on quantity purchases by corporations, associations, and others. For details, contact simplyyoupublishing@gmail.com

Table of Contents

PART ONE 1
CHAPTER 1: The Crux of Creativity
The Engine Behind Transformation 3

CHAPTER 2: Unknown Suppression
The Possible Danger of Fitting In 15

CHAPTER 3: Default Setting
Defining Your Comfort Zone 37

CHAPTER 4: Your Creativity
The Message of Your Itching Creative Gene 47

CHAPTER 5: Blown Lid
Breaking New Ground 59

PART TWO 69
CHAPTER 6: Living It!
It's Not a Diet; It's a Lifestyle! 71

CHAPTER 7: Doing It!
*Understanding the Steps
and Missteps of Living Creatively!* 87

CHAPTER 8: Monetizing It!
The Crafting and Reward cycle! 113

CHAPTER 9: Protecting It!
Create It, Own it, Keep it. 129

CHAPTER 10: In Conclusion
Live Your Legacy 141

ENDNOTES 153

Part One

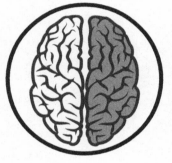

CHAPTER 1

The Crux of Creativity
The Engine Behind Transformation

"Your time is limited, so don't waste it living someone else's life. Don't be trapped by dogma — which is living with the results of other people's thinking. Don't let the noise of others' opinions drown out your own inner voice. And most important, have the courage to follow your heart and intuition." – Steve Jobs

Someone stole your creativity. Now is your chance to get it back.

At the perfect moment in a conversation or in a meeting, you held back your creative solution, instead making confessions and statements of regret, either to yourself or to others:

"I'm just not creative."

"I'm not sure if my idea is very good."

"I was just thinking the exact same thing."

"I thought of the same idea before, but I didn't think it would work."

"I was thinking along those lines, but I didn't want to be asked to explain it to others."

When someone was requesting help, perhaps you were the only one who understood their dilemma. It was your moment to offer a solution, or the idea that would lead to a solution. While others seemed stuck, you could see the dots connecting. But you were uncertain, or shy, or doubting yourself.

What if there was a way that your creativity could somehow transition from ideas to implementation? Or that the fear of your ideas being judged or considered crazy or impossible could disappear? Are you ready to take back your gift of creativity and live your life creatively? Would you like to externalize your imaginative thoughts? Are you tired of hiding your creative brilliance, or always giving it away for free?

Creativity needs to be an *intentional* force in your life.

It needs to be expressed and manifested. Your unique value to the world will not be complete without the inclusion of your creative genius. No longer should you allow your creative ideas to scare you or cause you to retreat to the safety of conformity when those ideas "pop" into your mind. Of course, your creativity need not always be expressed in raw form; it can be crafted or refined or discussed. But be *intentional* about your creativity.

ᥦ

The Creative Journey

The manifestation of creativity is a liberating journey; it takes you from a state of conformity and acceptance of the status quo to a state of uniqueness and intention. This journey can be described using the transitions below, and these serve as themes or influences for the chapters in this book.

From:	To:
Conformity	Consciousness
Terrified	Terrific
Admonition	Affirmation
Ideas	Implementation
Ridiculous	Reality

Enfeebled..Empowered

Tentative..Transformational

Vulnerable..Victorious

Implementation ....Intellectual Property

Yielding .... Being Yourself

Conformity is when you are pushed into areas and places that aren't right for you or aren't the best for you. You accept things as they are and you accept where you are—perhaps because of your academic performance on a test, your place of birth, your background or profession, and so many other factors. But it's time to blow the lid off and get to a place of **Consciousness** where you are alert, aware of your unique identity, and willing to give your best to the endless opportunities around you. A place where the limitations on your creativity and imagination are removed, and you shift from self-editing to the full exploration and expression of your creative ideas. A place where you refuse to simply accept the limitations and barriers in front of you and lead your life creatively.

Terrified is how you may feel when thinking about expressing your ideas and your creativity, even when you have accepted the fact that you are creative but even more so when you are yet to come to that realization. We live in a performance-based society, and thus the fear of rejection, of failing, or of not being accepted due to divergent thinking, can lead to isolation. But when you blow the lid off and let your light shine brightly, you not only illuminate new possibilities for others, you also enter a new realm of your life—which is absolutely Terrific.

Admonition may have been the main response your creativity has received when you have stepped out of the box. Your divergent thoughts and actions may have been rebuffed because they didn't conform to the norm. And this has resulted in you burying your ideas. You will thus have to create a new environment that supports your creative endeavors. A place where you can receive *Affirmation* for your uniqueness—surrounded by people who will help you affirm that you are indeed different and special. Your *Affirmation* will occur when you let your light shine and allow others to be guided by your light. And this *Affirmation* must be preceded by action, the action of blowing the lid off.

Ideation to *Implementation* is the journey that you are on. Ignite the idea!. Light it up! Implement it!

Ridiculous is what conformists will use to describe your imaginative thoughts and ideas. It may also be your own self-declaration when you view your life with a conformist lens. But when you blow the lid off and let your light shine, you shift to a place where those "ridiculous" ideas become *Reality*. Not just a reality for you but for so many others who have been waiting. In the '50s, the idea to place a man on the moon was not just ridiculous but absolutely ridiculous. That idea became reality and ushered in a new era for mankind.

Enfeebled represents the state of a suppressed creative gene. The force exerted by the lid has resulted in a lack of brightness and a lack of distinctness when it comes to your value. This then results in your creativity being squeezed back into the box of conformity. You lack the confidence to step out and be truly you. You may then become selective in applying your creativity, but when you blow the lid off, you experience *Empowerment*—the power to be truly and unapologetically you. You recognize your uniqueness and live a more fulfilling life, breaking through any stuck points and insecurities. You gain the courage to take back your hidden creativity. One thing I do during my training sessions, workshops, or keynote speeches is to ask participants what they would be doing instead of their current job if they had that option. As the participants search within, their facial expressions tell it all.

Some are hard pressed to come up with something because those ideas are buried, but with guidance they eventually come up with an idea, a life that absolutely lights them up.

Tentative is a place, or a concept, or a room that is cushioned with a lack of confidence and spread with sheets of self-doubt. Creativity, on the other hand, is not just an abstract concept and it's not a skill to be learned. Rather, it's a *Transformative* force. *Transformation* occurs when you blow the lid off. The shifting of energy fuels the lighting of your lantern. To blow the lid off requires a big change in your life, a *Transformation*.

The *Vulnerable* valley is the place you need to pass through in order to ascend to the *Victorious* mountain top. To blow the lid off is to reveal the fantastic ideas that you previously had no access to. It requires having confidence in your art, or your idea, or your offering, confidence that it is valuable and worthy. But the only way to truly let your light shine is to do so from Victory Mountain. Victory Mountain represents the ascent from self-doubt and self-editing to self-expression. It's the conquering of fear and the crushing of the irritating imposter syndrome; it's the summit of revelation and acceptance. So don't stay in the vulnerable valley; get up, move, step, run, silence the noise of the imposter syndrome fly and blow the lid off!

Implementation to *Intellectual Property* is what the creative journey entails. It's an asset that is yours, that you share with the world. That is how you let your light shine! It's your light, but many others will benefit from your light. Protect your light but never cover it up.

Finally, you will move away from *Yielding* to the pressure of the lid. From *Yielding* to the limitations and constraints on your creativity and your imagination. From allowing others to take away your creativity. Once you blow the lid off, you give yourself permission to simply be *You* unapologetically—to be *Yourself* and love *Yourself!*

You will not be defined by your profession, or aptitude, or test results, or executive position. You will be *Yourself!*

I don't define myself by my skills, or my profession, or my education, or my position. Personally, I like to define myself by my three key pillars that I affectionately call CAP:

Champion for Creativity
Ambassador for Wellness
Pursuer of Excellence

The support for harnessing and unlocking creativity is growing, but it requires the inclusion of more participants and more advocates. The message is that creativity is not an abstract concept but an integral and critical part of life.

Creativity is not a luxury in our lives; it is a necessity.

Our constantly evolving times are nourished by creative ideas, and many people are missing out on the opportunity that these changes bring because their "creative gene" is being suppressed. The desire to live a unique life filled with purpose may be slipping away from them. What the next generation requires is acceptance that being different or not fitting with the norm are not bad things; being different can lead to creativity, inventions, progress...Creativity is a critical life skill.

"Creativity is highly important for the economic, social, and personal welfare of people in the modern Western society."[2]

The United Nations has been advocating for more recognition and support for creative industries. In 2017, a UN resolution[3]

[1] Cropley, A.J. (2014). "Neglect of creativity in education: A moral issue." In S. Moran, D.H. Cropley & J.C. Kaufman (Eds.), The ethics of creativity (pp. 250–264). New York: Palgrave Macmillan.

[2] Tan, O.S. (2015). "Flourishing creativity: Education in an age of wonder." Asia Pacific Education Review, 16, 161–166. https://doi.org/10.1007/s12564-015-9377-6.

[3] United Nations. General Assembly. 71/284-World Creativity and Innovation Day. April 27, 2017.

officially set aside April 21 to celebrate creativity and innovation (six days after Leonardo da Vinci's birthday). Also, there is a call for creative industries to be included in economic planning.[4] Creativity has both commercial and cultural value; it catalyzes change and builds more inclusive, connected, and collaborative societies.[5] Cultural and creative industries (CCI) generate $2.25 billion of revenue globally (exceeding those of telecom services at $1.57 billion globally) and create 29.5 million jobs worldwide. The world is at one of its most innovative and creative times, and creativity is being discussed everywhere, from the boardroom to the classroom. The thought of autonomous means of transport being our automotive future or the extinction of many traditional careers and the creation of unconventional ones are no longer considered farfetched. Not that many years ago, nobody would have guessed that one could have a career managing social media pages.

The World Economic Forum (WEF), in its *Future of Jobs Report 2018,* projects that many traditional roles such as accounting, bookkeeping, payroll clerks, and bank tellers, among others, will become extinct; while new roles such as digital marketing and strategy specialists, big data specialists, and process automation specialists are where the future of jobs lie. The report also shows that **creativity** is the number one upcoming skill and will be the third most important skill to have by 2020 (preceded only by **critical thinking** and **complex problem solving**). More and more people are thinking outside of, and even crushing, the box by thinking and creating on a whole new level. YouTube™ sensations are appearing daily because people are more appreciative and attuned to creative ideas and innovative solutions.

Employers the world over are some of the biggest proponents

---

[4] United Nations Conference on Trade and Development. Creative Economic Outlook Report.
[5] Ernest & Young, "Cultural Times, The first global map of cultural and creative industries," December 2015.

of creativity and the encouragement of employees to embrace creativity. Considerable efforts are being made to provide working environments that are conducive to encouraging employees to brainstorm and challenge the status quo. The biggest and most profitable global companies of our time (such as Google and Apple) are now dropping college degree requirements (even in my accountancy field, e.g., Ernest & Young) in exchange for proprietors of uniqueness, creativity, and innovation. This is reflective of a 2013[6] Georgetown University study, which showed that by 2020, 36% of job openings will not require education beyond high school. However, a large number of employers are still not open to, or equipped to handle, the creative ideas of their employees.

LinkedIn's Economic Graph data revealed in early 2019 that creativity is the most in-demand skill in the world. Process-driven jobs are disappearing and employees need to demonstrate creative thinking. Their report states that mastering creativity will benefit the rest of your career, regardless of your field or discipline, as it will become even more important moving forward.

The [7]ACCA (Association of Chartered Certified Accountants), for example, commissioned a report "The Drivers of Change and Future Skills" to explore the likely changes that will impact the accountant of the future, and what skills will be required to remain relevant beyond 2020. Echoing the WEF Future Jobs report, the study showed the traditional role of the accountant quickly diminishing. The report suggests that to remain relevant, the accountant should have seven key "quotients" for success. The more obvious skills ranked lower, while creativity was one of the highly ranked skills required for the accountant to achieve success in the future environment.

Despite this new creative movement brought about by the

---

[6] Georgetown University, "Recovery: Job Growth and Education Requirements Through 2020," 2014.

[7] ACCA, "Drivers of change and future skills," June 2016.

Fourth Industrial Revolution and the rise of AI (Artificial Intelligence), the vast majority of employees are not tapping into their creativity—one of the key future currencies and differentiators. Many transformational ideas pop into our brains and are nullified daily. The limitless potential solutions to many of our current problems are often not even being discussed because of the suppression of our creativity. People are seemingly afraid to truly be themselves and instead focus their attention on societal norms or celebrity influence. Being different or unique seems to be less and less appreciated; and those who are deemed creative are not seeing the fruits of their labor and are not able to fully monetize their creative work.

To be creative or productive?

Adobe's "State of Create: 2016" report examined what they call the "Creativity Gap." This report showed that unlocking creativity was critical to economic growth, according to 64% of respondents; while in 2012, 80% of respondents deemed it critical. In 2016, 70% felt that creativity was valuable to society, yet a striking minority (31%) believed that they were living up to their own creative potential.

This clash between productivity and creativity seems to also be represented by the left-brain/right-brain clash. The resounding message is that to be productive, you must put away creativity, which means creativity is being "taken away" from us; it is being held captive. But we are here to liberate it, to blow the lid off!

Nonetheless, the report showed that companies that embrace creativity are number one in their field and tend to be the best companies to work for. Fifty percent of Americans consider themselves to be creative, while the percentage drops to 39% for the rest of the world. The IBM Capitalizing on Complexity research involving 5,000 CEOs showed that creativity is key to remaining relevant and is the most important leadership characteristic; yet

75% of the employees of those companies reported that they are under growing pressure to be more productive rather than more creative. As noted, the "State of Create" report echoes this, with 77% of respondents reporting that they are pressured to be productive, despite 56% reporting that there is an increasing need to be more creative.

How This Book Works

Blow the Lid Off! will help you blow the lid off your creative limitations and give you the confidence to live creatively and enhance your value. Transform your life and affirm your uniqueness and true value!

While this book takes you through a journey of how to blow the lid off and live your crazy, creative life, it is, in essence, a series of pictures of my own journey. I wrote this book to you and for you, as I understand how you might be feeling—your experience of not quite fitting in, of seemingly appearing crazy when you share your ideas, and thus having to suppress or cover up the true creative side of yourself. A part of you wishes to be seen and heard, and to be able to express yourself fully, but fear yanks you back into its cage. I understand that you need some encouragement and guidance to step out and move forward, to burst through the barriers in your path, and live your crazy, creative life happily.

There are those who are eagerly awaiting your creative solutions. The liberation of your creativity cannot be put on hold any longer. It's time to set it free!

Here, you will learn how to turn your crazy, creative ideas into a form that can be consumed and appreciated by others. You will be guided on how to use your creativity and how to protect it.

This book is divided into two parts. Part 1 is introspective and thought-provoking, and it challenges the status quo regarding creativity. It relates to the right hemisphere—the creative side—of our brain. Part 2 shifts to the left hemisphere—the logical side—and it offers practical steps and tools that you can use to shape your creativity and offer your gifts to the world.

Each chapter opens with a story and a quotation to encourage intentional thinking and to provide a base for discussion through analogies. Being a book of the NOW, each chapter has a page for you to write your notes and record the steps you will need to take in your journey.

You can also share your progress on social media using the hashtag #BlowTheLidOff, and you can find more information at my website: www.robertabelle.com.

On this adventure, give your excitement and your imagination room to grow. Stay focused on the content you are consuming and dig deep.

Your passion and your mission will be clearer by the end of this book, and you will be prepared to blast off into living your new creative life. Enjoy this journey by being open-minded and focusing on your personal life experiences and awakenings.

When you are finished reading this book, you will have an enhanced mindset. You will understand that creativity extends beyond artistry into scholarly areas and everyday life. You will proudly and boldly declare yourself as creative, and you will see the value and benefits that your creative light has for the lives of others. You will get the best of both worlds and both brain hemispheres by theorizing and applying creativity.

NOTES

_____

_____

_____

_____

_____

_____

_____

_____

_____

_____

_____

_____

_____

_____

_____

_____

CHAPTER 2

Unknown Suppression
The Possible Danger of Fitting In

> *"Creativity is not just about art – it is one of the most crucial human traits. It lies at the heart of innovation; thus it is not a superficial skill but a necessity for human survival."* – **Balder Onarheim, PhD**

Creativity is about more than generating ideas—and simply being different is not enough to be genuinely creative.

Creativity is the development and crafting of imaginative thoughts and ideas expressed outwardly, and it is useful for the situations from which it is generated. Creativity must be relevant by adding value to existing issues. Creativity is not just about coming up with different answers to a question but coming up with different questions and then looking for the answers.

Creativity is a fundamental activity of human information processing.[8] It is generally agreed to include two defining characteristics: "…the ability to produce work that is both novel (i.e., original, unexpected) and appropriate (i.e., useful, adaptive concerning task constraints)" (Sternberg & Lubart, 1999, p. 3).[9] "By defini-

---

[8] Boden, J. E., & Boden, G. M. (1969). "The other side of the brain III: The corpus callosum and creativity." Bulletin of the Los Angeles Neurological Society, 34, 191-203.

[9] Sternberg, R. J., & Lubart, T. I. (1999). "The concept of creativity: Prospects and paradigms." In R. J. Sternberg (Ed.), *Handbook of creativity* (pp. 3-15). Cambridge: Cambridge University Press.

tion, creative insights occur in consciousness. When creativity is the result of deliberate control, as opposed to spontaneous generation, the prefrontal cortex also instigates the creative process. Both processing modes, deliberate and spontaneous, can guide neural computation in structures that contribute emotional content and in structures that provide cognitive analysis, yielding the four basic types of creativity."[10] You must get to that state of consciousness to unlock your creativity; you must take the journey from simply seeing things as they are to seeing things as they could be and where you could be. The journey must start here.

The [11]**Four-C Model of Creativity** describes four levels of creativity as follows:

Mini-c: …is inherent in learning and occurs when one attempts a new task. Ideas and insights are new to the individual and thus need not be shared with anyone or receive validation or acknowledgement. At this level, creative ability is visible, however, not sufficient for creative performance. "One must have the confidence and willingness to express and develop their creative ideas."[12]

Little-c: Here, the act of sharing creative ideas and receiving appropriate feedback helps more than just the creator. Solutions to everyday problems are achieved by helping people adapt to changing environments. The spark and the light begin to benefit others.

Pro-c: The desire to go fully into one's creative passions occurs at this level. One becomes a professional after years of study in the arts or related fields. The goal with this type of creativity goes be-

---

[10] Arne Dietrich, "The cognitive neuroscience of creativity," *Psychonomic Bulletin & Review*, 11 (6), 1011, 2004.

[11] Helfand, M., Kaufman, J. C., & Beghetto, R. A. (2017). "The Four C Model of Creativity: Culture and Context." In V. P. Glăveanu (Ed.), Palgrave handbook of creativity and culture research (pp. 15-360). New York: Palgrave.

[12] Helfand, M., Kaufman, J. C., & Beghetto, R. A. (2017). "The Four C Model of Creativity: Culture and Context." In V. P. Glăveanu (Ed.), Palgrave handbook of creativity and culture research (p. 19). New York: Palgrave.

yond just helping others and includes making a living from one's creative pursuits. Persons at this level seek to make creativity their "full-time job."

Big-C: At this final level, the creative person becomes respected or eminent in their field. Their particular form of creativity may lead to ground-breaking discoveries, "household name" status, or global accolades, such as the Nobel Peace Prize.

The answer to the looming question of whether creativity is a result of nature or nurture is that it is both. Creativity is not an either/or trait. The nature-nurture relationship is best described as a continuum. Even if you are not fully convinced that you are innately creative, that is not a problem at this moment. I want you to at least know that we all have a "creative gene" which can often be suppressed as we grow and live our lives. Its expression may have been "taken away from you." Humans have a great deal of intentional control over what they attend to, and the attentional network of the prefrontal cortex is not only a mechanism to select the content of consciousness[13] [14] but also to maintain the chosen content online long enough for a creative solution to mature.

಄

What Is This "Creative Gene?"

There is no conclusive evidence that we have a gene specifically for creativity in our DNA. Research shows, however, that several specific genes play a key role in the generation of creativity[15]

---

[13] Cowan N. "Attention and memory: An integrated framework." New York, NY, US: Oxford University Press; 1995.
[14] Posner MI, Dehaene S. "Attentional networks." Trends Neurosci. 1994 Feb;17(2):75–79.
[15] Helfand, M., Kaufman, J. C., & Beghetto, R. A. (2017). "The Four C Model of Creativity: Culture and Context." In V. P. Glăveanu (Ed.), *Palgrave handbook of creativity and culture research* (pp. 15-360). New York: Palgrave.

As more research is conducted to investigate the biological basis of creativity, I have taken the position that every human being possesses creativity—a "creative gene,"—which is a result of complex genetics. There are various models regarding the stages of creativity but popular preference points to the four-step process model, such as the one described by the Wallis mode of creative process: Preparation, Incubation, Illumination, and Verification. Personally, I like to collapse the steps into two broad steps for the purpose of simplicity. The steps then are **Imagination** and **Expression**.

Creativity must begin with ideas and insights but must be followed by the creative response of expression. Journeying to the state of consciousness will: 1) help you recognize the existence of your creative gene, and 2) activate your creative gene to a point of expression.

I liken this process (in a simplistic manner) to the two main stages of gene expression: transcription, where the production and processing of the DNA messengers occurs, and translation, where the utilization and expression of the message occurs.

❧

Suppressing the Creative Gene

Abraham Maslow, a major contributor to the field of psychology, observed this similarly. After studying renowned artists such as Mozart and Picasso, he said it was clear that they had a special creative characteristic. However, he concluded that the creative characteristic is universal to every human being, "The creativeness of the self-actualized man seems rather to be kin to the naïve and universal creativeness of unspoiled children. It seems to be more a fundamental characteristic of common human nature, a potentiality given to all human beings at birth. Most human beings lose this as they become enculturated, but some individuals seem either to retain this fresh, naïve, and direct way of looking at life; or if they have lost it, as most people do, they later in life recover it."[16]

The environment in which you live and grow can lead to the suppression of your creative gene. Here you may find yourself somewhere on the continuum between not even thinking about creative ideas (suppression at the transcription/imagination stage) or considering yourself creative and having great ideas but not outwardly expressing them (suppression at the translation/expression stage). Depending on your environmental persuasion, your creativity may be in danger by virtue of "fitting in." You may be required to conform to an existing culture. If this culture does not support your creative expressions, it may give rise to behaviors that are incompatible with the creative process. Thus, a fight ensues between creativity and conformity—more pressure on the lid that has been placed on your creativity. You're confined to the reality around you. You become convinced that you were not born creative, that your toolkit of skills does not include creativity, perhaps because you believe you are not artistic or you have not received a certification to boost your confidence in your creative abilities.

❧

While planning to take its innovation to a new level, NASA sought to test the creative potential of its rocket scientists and engineers. Drs. George Land and Beth Jarman developed a longitudinal test of creative potential. They later decided to test this on 1,600 school children age four to five. The test results revealed that the children scored at a shocking creative genius level of 98%. They continually tested the children as they progressed through school and into adulthood. The results showed that creativity is

---

[16] Maslow, Abraham. *Motivation and Personality.* New York: Harper & Brothers, 1954.

not something we learn but rather something we unlearn. "Non-creative behavior is learned," states Dr. Land.

The results below show that at the age of 25 years and older, only 2% of this group were able to score a creative genius level score.

Age at testing	Number tested	Year of testing	Percent who scored in the "highly creative" range
5 years	1,600 children	1968	98%
10 years	1,600 children	1978	30%
15 years	1,600 children	1983	12%
25+ years	280,000 adults	1985	2%

While "fitting in" achieves success regarding educational and career advancements, it fails to promote creativity by suppressing our creative gene. Maslow states that the creativity of childhood "diminishes due to a superficial but powerful set of inhibitions" that keeps one's creativity in check.

My eldest daughter, Jahzara Jewel, is now five years old and she has revealed her first "what I want to be when I grow up" statement. Currently at her 98% highly creative genius phase (see above), she told me with strong conviction, "Dad, I want to be an astronaut and go to the moon in outer space." My shocked but happy response was simply, "Great, let's work on it." I followed up with inquiries regarding her possible interest in traditional professions such as becoming a doctor or lawyer or working in law enforcement. Expecting her to desire these professions also, she simply told me that someone else could do them; she wanted to focus on going to the moon.

Therefore, when her school sent out an email that there would be a digital portable planetarium (the only one in the East African region) onsite to showcase a space and astro show and expose students to outer space, I was the first person to register. Leading up to the event, she didn't seem to be as excited as I had expected. I figured that perhaps her interest had died down and her dreams were coming back to earth.

However, as soon as I got home that evening, I was met at the door with my daughter's absolute joy and excitement. "Daddy, do you know that today I went into space, like for real. I went into space and I saw many planets and how stars are formed—it was awesome!" It was the highlight of the year for her, and she often talked to me about the experience. I had the feeling that it was probably hard for her to find someone else who would understand her excitement about her "astronaut" experience.

During the progress meeting with her teachers at the end of the school term, I told them that her space experience was her absolute favorite, and I mentioned her desire to be an astronaut. They quickly understood because it explained why most of her drawings and artwork consisted of the sun, planets, or stars.

It's interesting to note that when my daughter was 18-months-old, I created a routine where after dinner we would go for a night stroll around the neighborhood and she would look at the sky. Who knows? Perhaps, this contributed to her lunar desires.

At this point in her life, she still wants to be an astronaut and land on the moon. I have, therefore, made a commitment to support her creative genius by exposing her to experiences and knowledge relevant to this desire. For example, I have organized for her and some of her friends to visit the space center in Kenya so as to give her more practical knowledge. I am also cognizant that her career aspirations are likely to change as she grows older, but I will not allow this change to be as a result of the suppression of her creativity and her aspirations.

There are several factors that can lead to the suppression of one's creative gene. Let's look at these factors and how they can suppress our creative thinking, even without us knowing it.

༄

External Suppression Factors

1. Family Orientation and Culture:

The family unit is where the values, beliefs, and norms of a child are developed and molded. Just as your outlook on relationships, work, money, and other aspects of life are learned from your family members, so is your approach to creativity.

How does your family interact with creativity? Do you have open conversations about creativity? As a parent, what role does creativity play in your family's daily life? Is your response to your children's creativity similar to your parents' response? Does your family's definition of success include aspects of creativity?

Culture establishes a threshold not only for our creativity but also for the creativity of others. Conversations around the pursuit of success need to also factor in the expression of creativity. Misguided expressions of creativity must be handled with care, particularly for children at an early age, when their imagination is endless and raw.

The harnessing of our children's creative brilliance should be done with intent, while recognizing that creativity, like personality, is never a one-size-fits-all situation. Exposure to different cultures can be an important aspect in the development of creativity, so we must ensure that they have an appreciation of and respect for other cultures.

A new sofa arrived in our house and before the dust could settle, I came home to a report that my eldest child (the astronaut in waiting) had written on the sofa! As I was taught, property is to be respected and cared for. While this is a great lesson to learn, I reminded myself that I needed to avoid suppressing my children's creativity. My initial reactions were of anger and disappointment, but I had to ensure that I didn't react only negatively to the situation.

While reflecting on my next move, I recalled that my daughter had previously written on a wall and I had made her scrub it off. Ever since that talk, she had not drawn on the walls. So it dawned on me that I perhaps should have communicated the fact to her that not only was writing on walls wrong, so was writing on furniture. At this moment, I still had not looked at the sofa, and I presumed it just had a few scribbles.

But to my utter surprise, my child had drawn people images on the sofa! I inquired about the meaning of the images versus why she did it—which would typically be my first question—and she explained that she was feeling lonely that day and wanted to draw her family on the sofa, imagining them sitting on the sofa and keeping her company.

The ball of anger I was harboring immediately disappeared and it was replaced with the appreciation of a proud parent. Later, I spoke to her sharing my appreciation for the creativity in her art and also reminding her of our previous conversation about writing on the walls. This time, I communicated the need to respect furniture and other household property, and we talked about what were considered acceptable places for writing and drawing.

I learned a great lesson regarding how often, as a parent, I am quick to dispense punitive responses to infringements, as opposed to pausing, reflecting, and responding in a more understanding manner. I had to remind myself to be more mindful in my parenting, instead of rushing through life and seeing my children's need for my attention as an interruption. Allowing her the freedom to express herself and scheduling quality time for her is paramount for the development of her personality, which, in turn, helps in the nurturance of her creative potential and problem-solving skills.

"Parenting that provides opportunities for imagination, play, self-expression, and divergent thinking fosters creative thinking and problem solving."[17] [18] [19]

I also promised to ensure that she always had drawing paper on hand so she could express herself by drawing. She holds me accountable to this promise and always notifies me when her art supplies are running low. "Daddy, please bring me more writing books when you come back home, okay?" Whenever I have extra writing pads, notebooks, or journals from conferences, I give them to her. I also use her work to check out the stages of her creative development.

Nonetheless, one day she proudly wrote her name on the living room wall to show me her writing skills. "Daddy, the wall was so dull and plain, but I wrote my name so nicely for everyone to see," she told me.

After all, who said that house walls should be plain and dull with just one color? We had a tradition in high school that on the last official day of our final year, we would sign our shirts and write all over them to be kept as memorabilia. As children, we may have had bedrooms with various wallpapers and posters, and perhaps our best artwork from school or home, and then we transition into adulthood and our walls become plain and blank. But instead of

---

[17] Runco, M. A. Problem finding, problem solving, and creativity. California: Greenwood Publishing Group, 1994.

[18] Vandenberg, B, "Problem-solving and creativity," In K.H. Rubin (Ed.), New Directions for Child Development: Children's Play. San Fransisco: Jossey-Bass, 1980.

[19] Striker, Susan. Young at Art: Teaching Toddlers Self-Expression, Problem-Solving Skills, and an Appreciation for Art. New York: Holt, Henry & Company, Inc., 2001.

brightening them up with appropriate content, we simply leave them unadorned, as if to signal the end of creativity in our lives and the beginning of moving on to conformity.

The creativity of our childhood gets forgotten, the creative gene gets suppressed, and creative expression is minimized. As an adult, life is too serious to be interrupted by creative expression and productivity gets our undivided support due to the "seriousness of life."

℘

2. Formal Education

If you grew up like I did, you were taught that the pathway to a successful life was to get a good education, land a solid job, get married, and live happily ever after. There would be very little room for creativity unless the subject was art or music. No wonder we think that creativity is only for artists and musicians. But the truth is that we can be both productive and creative at the same time and in many, many different ways.

The education system assesses performance based on the results of standardized tests and various types of exams. As with many students, the thought of examinations would cause immense fear in my body. Since then, I've observed how examinations have progressed in an attempt to bring about a more balanced approach to assessment. However, these improvements are still ineffective in identifying and leveraging a student's abilities and creative talents. Educators are hard pressed to ensure that the syllabus is delivered within a specific timeframe, and examination results are regarded as the key determinant to measure the performance of not just the student but also the teacher and the learning institution. One's progression and success through the entire education system is then based on grades and test results.

Test anxiety rises sharply in students in Grades 2 to 4, and it remains high as they move through middle school and high school. Although estimates vary, about 20% of students appear to have truly severe test anxiety, while another 16% of students might be considered to have moderately high test anxiety. An estimated 10 million children are affected in North America alone, and test anxiety appears to be increasing with the growing national emphasis on standardized testing. According to the American Test Anxieties Association (yes, there is such a thing!), "schoolwork" and "exams" are reported by students as the most stressful things in their lives.[20]

We live in a test-conscious, test-giving culture in which the lives of people are in part determined by their test performance.[21]

The goal in the earlier stages of education is to ensure that you grasp and can apply subject matter concepts, thus diminishing room for questions or deviating from the standard. Time for questioning and reflection will be afforded to you at the high school level (if at all) or at the tertiary level. However, even at the tertiary level, there exists the pressure to obtain good grades as the pathway to success and to avoid the high levels of unemployment. The cycle is thus perpetuated, leaving very little room for thinking outside the box. There is so much more focus on percentiles and placements rather than on engagement or sparking inspiration and creativity.

When I was in primary school, as our spelling abilities were being developed, we would be given a list of 14 words every Monday and then tested on the same words Tuesday morning. Easy, right? I consistently got grades of either 0/14 or 2/14. My reward was punishment and extra words to learn and to be tested on because failing the test was a clear indication that I was not working hard

---

[20] "Test Anxiety," American Test Anxieties Association, http://amtaa.org.
[21] Sarason, S.B., Davidson, K.S., Lighthall, F.F. et al. Anxiety in elementary school children. New York: Wiley, 1960.

enough. It turns out that I was dyslexic, but at that time, neither teachers nor parents had the knowledge to recognize dyslexia. To date, I still have difficulties with spelling but I know creative ways to avoid common mistakes.

The limitation here is that the system was not able to identify the unique needs of each student and therefore couldn't adjust the learning to suit an individual's particular needs. And unfortunately, deviations from the standard were met with various forms of punishment. Nowadays, conditions like dyslexia are better understood, but there still needs to be more emphasis on how different students learn and how each student's particular gifts and skills can be better utilized.

The education system has not been good at recognizing and utilizing the richness of alternatives through divergence. Divergent thinking relies on a state of consciousness that explores various possibilities. The creative journey will move on from the twin state of convergent thinking and conformity to the liberating twin state of divergent thinking and consciousness.

The Future of Jobs Report 2018 reveals that "the inherent opportunities for economic prosperity, societal progress, and individual flourishing in this new world of work are enormous yet depend crucially on the ability of all concerned stakeholders to instigate reform in places such as education." In this report, 65% of respondents stated that their creativity was being stifled by the education system.

The idea of "divergent thinking" was first proposed by the American psychologist J.P. Guilford (one of the founders of the Theories of Creativity) [22] in the 1950s when he noticed that creative people tended more toward divergent thinking, thus associating

---

[22] Wikipedia contributors, "J. P. Guilford," Wikipedia, *The Free Encyclopedia*, https://en.wikipedia.org/w/index.php?title=J._P._Guilford&oldid=914820318 (accessed October 24, 2019).

creativity with divergent thinking. According to Runco and Jae-ger (2012), divergent thinking is a catalyst for creativity, but they note that it is not synonymous with creativity—because creativity requires ideas that are both different and effective.

My high school education proved to be a more positive experience. I had always considered myself different, and in a formal education system, being different typically got you labelled as a problem child. However, one of my teachers refused to use that label and saw me for the unique student that I was. He understood that "different" simply meant different, not wrong or bad. Based on the standard approach to a child in my particular situation at that time, he was expected to punish me by cutting my break time and giving me extra work to do. During such times of "punishment," however, he would have conversations with me to gain a better understanding of what was the best way to help me learn. How he figured that out, I still don't know.

What I do know is that I learn a lot faster and easier through conversations and challenging concepts. My teacher designed a unique type of program to help me learn and this greatly improved my performance. While the class would be on topic 3 for instance, I would already be on topic 12. I later came to understand that he shifted my education to a student-driven learning approach, and the results were dramatic!

A student-driven learning approach involves building the student's skills to enable the student to learn and problem solve using their unique style, instead of relying on a teacher-driven approach and memorization. I also discovered that I had a strong photographic memory, which is a great talent to have. I went on to perform well on my SATs (Scholastic Aptitude Tests), thus attracting the attention of several colleges. I also received an invitation to attend the Global Young Leaders Conference, which was a conference for exceptional high school students to gain first hand exposure to international diplomacy and to be exposed to global cultures and perspectives in order to take leadership positions and make impactful decisions.

In Kenya, the body mandated to review the education curriculum is the Kenya Institute of Curriculum Development (KICD). After reviewing the existing education system and identifying the gaps and shortfalls, KICD produced a report in 2017 entitled Basic Education Curriculum Framework. In the report, it was acknowledged that the current education system's curriculum content (it was called 8-4-4) and its implementation were academic and examination oriented. The curriculum, due to an over reliance on examinations, made little provision for the recognition of the learner's potential gifts and talents—thus contributing to increased dropout rates and high unemployment. (Kenya's unemployment rate in 2017 was 39.1%.)[23] Now one of the core competencies of the new education system is to develop the students' creativity and imagination.

In the past, someone who had performed exceptionally well in their academic subjects might well be urged not to transition into a creative field as that would be a waste of intellect. And yet creativity requires intellect. Think of the great inventors, scientists, and geniuses of the world. What they had in common was a combination of intellect and creativity.

During a workshop for teachers in which I was invited to speak on the theme of "Reshaping Education," I challenged the educators by stating that in an age driven by data and technology, and ready access to information, what students need most is connection. Connection to the material that is being presented (its relevance and applicability), connection to the teacher as a facilitator of learning and not a military drill sergeant who gives commands and instructions, and connection to their purpose and destiny so

---

[23] United Nations Development Programme, "Human Development Index (HDI)," *Human Development Reports*, 2017.

that the student can begin to find his way in life and be equipped to navigate the terrain of misinformation.

Education is the process of facilitating the acquisition of knowledge and the application of that knowledge along with relevant values and principles. What needs redefining is the method. Students should leave school with a solid grasp of where they fit in this grand picture of life, instead of just wondering which job or company they will work for—that is secondary.

"School rewards people for their memory. Life rewards people for their imagination. School rewards caution; life rewards daring. Make the world your classroom and not the classroom your world." – Anonymous

ఴ

3. Integration into Society

There exists a glaring limitation in society, in that we have become socialized to focus on right-doing rather than right-thinking. As a result, questioning the status quo may at times be interpreted as an act of rebellion. Then we fall back in line to fit in and carefully tuck away any ideas that are contrary to existing patterns. While the process of ensuring harmony is important, the manner in which this happens can lead to the unfortunate suppression of our creative gene.

The appetite for risk and adventure, the respect for the rule of law, and many other attributes and attitudes that we have as individuals are typically strengthened or weakened according to the society in which we live. How does your society relate to creativity? Are creatives in your community honored or are they typically rejected? What funding opportunities exist for creative endeavors? What copyright protection mechanisms exist to protect creators such as authors and artists?

Regardless of a nation's main GDP contributor, creativity can be incorporated into it, often with impressive results.

How much government and civil society support do the Cultural and Creative Industries (CCIs) receive in your country? Content is king; content creation is what drives the digital economy. We cannot accept digital disruption without a rich appreciation for creativity. Imagine your digital device without streaming services or social media applications that only include news items!

A community that fails to recognize, integrate, and appreciate creativity is one that contributes to the suppression of the creative gene. As mentioned earlier, employers are dropping degree requirements and instead favoring creativity and innovation. On the other hand, a large number of employers have yet to adopt this mindset.

Also, creativity is often the spark for economic development and for societal advancement and improvement. Referring back to the IBM report, it says, "All around us are matters of national and international importance that are crying out for creative solutions…" Nevertheless, funding for creative endeavors is typically less than for other areas, and it is typically the first area to be cut in times of economic downturn.

The aforementioned suppression factors are institutionally based barriers. They affect the manner in which we perceive and interact with creativity. And a poor creative climate can configure our thinking to not be creative.

So what else could be suppressing our creative potential?

છ

Attitudinal Suppression Factors

Author Roger Von Oech states that we can get by in life without being creative, given that our routine tasks such as driving, shopping, and communicating do not require creative thinking. In his book, A Whack on the Side of the Head, he identifies 10 mental blocks that further suppress our creativity. The mental blocks according to Von Oech are:

1. *The Right Answer:* When we think there is only one right answer, we keep quiet for fear of being wrong and lock out possibilities for innovative thinking.

2. *That's Not Logical:* Trying to rationalize creative ideas hinders creative ideas, as it fails to recognize that illogical thinking is beneficial.

3. *Follow the Rules:* Rule following fails to see things as they could be but instead focuses on how they currently are.

4. *Be Practical:* Practicality does not allow for the pursuit of "what if" scenarios.

5. *Play Is Frivolous:* Creative output is often the result of playing with ideas using our five-year-old creative intuition.

6. *That's Not My Area:* This excuse robs us of the rich opportunity to get inspiration from other fields and to broaden our horizons.

7. *Don't Be Foolish:* Conforming to the norm and yielding to peer pressure traps us in "group thinking" creating a conformist environment in which creativity cannot grow.

8. *Avoid Ambiguity:* Too much specificity can stifle your imagination, thus preventing you from exploring anything beyond your typical boundaries.

9. *To Err Is Wrong:* Mastering the art of being wrong or failing can ultimately lead to creative results and new inventions.

10. *I'm Not Creative:* This one is a self-fulfilling prophecy—if

you believe it, you will be right. You are locking yourself in the proverbial box.

The journey of our creative life requires us to question what we have been taught about creativity and to leave the arena of limiting belief, "I can't because..."

While the digital revolution has made life very convenient, it has also led us to be distracted and absentminded as we go through life. We may tend to be more concerned with people and information online than who and what is right in front of us in real time. Is all this digital distraction contributing to the suppression of our creative gene? Are we losing the love of art and the meaning of art—the ability to look at the world with our imagination and our personal interpretation?

We need to ask ourselves how we can maintain a healthy balance.

While technology has invited more participants into the creative space (such as YouTube sensations), the creation of that content often happens off-line through brainstorming and reflection. You need time away from your digital devices to reflect on what you have consumed both digitally and non digitally.

Unstructured time can be a friend to creativity, and we should embrace it. We need to allow for unstructured "play" time to help us exercise our mental muscles so our creative genes can be fully expressed.

Being in a constant consuming mode hinders our dreaming ability. "Now that technology is capable of creating the stuff of our wildest dreams, designers have simply stopped dreaming," says Elliot Jay Stocks.

While technology has helped to make our dreams a reality, we still need to keep dreaming; it's always important to keep dreaming.

Consider two "worlds" for a moment: the REAL world and the DREAM world.

The real world is where we exist and we cannot deny its existence—such as the device or book you are reading, the chair you are sitting on, the air you are breathing. However, it is a world that is full of *repetition* and routines, and if they are not adjusted over time, they can become *exhausting* and *entrenched*. And when we live only in our routines, we may not be able to imagine things or even our lives in general being different such that the mention or thought of a change can lead us to become hesitant or *afraid*. Then our world gets filled with *limitations* and we are not able to see beyond what currently exists. This is why creative thoughts and ideas can sometimes be met with limiting statements like, "Well, I live in the real world!" or "What world do you live in?"

Well I don't live in the REAL world, I simply exist here. I live in the DREAM world and use my creativity to manifest those dreams and make them reality.

Perhaps, this is a deconstruction of statements such as "I am just not creative." I am an accountant so that is all there is to me. A creative accountant? No, that just doesn't exist.

But when we live in the DREAM world, our imaginations become alive. This is a place of *Discovery* that *Revolutionizes* the REAL world. It is a place that *Energizes* us as we see the dots connecting and forming an Alignment. This Alignment brings together and leverages our entire being—our experiences, our successes, our failures, (and not simply our profession or our test scores)—so that the REAL world simply becomes *Magnificent*!

YOU become magnificent!

You let your light shine!

"No matter where you are from, your dreams are valid."
– *Lupita Nyong'o*

Takeaways

Creativity occurs naturally in our lives. Creativity brings the color to life, and this is certainly not restricted to the arts and music. Creativity is everywhere.

Molding yourself to fit within the status quo can lead to the suppression of your creativity.

Hopefully, this hasn't happened to you. If it has, the good news is that this state is reversible. There are many people who have realized that this is not where they want to be—they want to express their creativity. Often, they discover that they have a specific talent, and they want to develop it and share it with the world.

As you examine your state of consciousness, identify your current state of creativity. Do you feel that your creative gene has been suppressed? If so, what are the factors of suppression?

Refuse to accept any limitations that have been placed upon you. Become a dreamer. When you blow the lid off, you defy the box that has confined your imagination and you give your creative gene room to express itself.

NOTES

CHAPTER 3

Default Setting
Defining Your Comfort Zone

*"The comfort zone is the great enemy to creativity;
moving beyond it necessitates intuition, which in
turn configures new perspectives and conquers fears."*
– **Dan Stevens**

Have you ever bought new electronics?

Consider the excitement and anticipation regarding the particular benefits and features. Two different users can derive various levels of performance and satisfaction from the same device as a result of each user's technical abilities and personal preferences, and each user can make different modifications to the device's default settings.

Many people never take the time to even look at the default settings of their smartphone. Could it be because we are used to accepting things just the way they are? Typically, most changes will be to their wallpaper or screensaver. However, the layout of the apps, the font style, and the notification settings are left undisturbed. The argument here is, "Why fix it if it isn't broken?"

Regarding our creative process, many of us tend to accept things just the way they are—typically not questioning or wondering what possibilities could exist or how things might be done more efficiently.

Understanding our default settings is the next progressive step in the process of unleashing creativity. Default settings define our comfort zone, which in turn establishes the outer boundaries to our creativity. Therefore, even if you were to blow the lid off and destroy the box, without changing your default settings you stand the risk of re-erecting those same walls that confined your creativity in the first place.

However, operating in a new environment can sometimes be uncomfortable or even terrifying. The creative journey is filled with uncertainty. I mean even the act of blowing the lid off can be terrifying. But the end results can be terrific—and exciting! Think about approaching the changes to your default settings with anticipation, with the idea of trying out some new configurations—your configurations. You can try out some new ideas and put your unique twist on things. Use your imagination and see what happens!

Perhaps, one of the most terrifying aspects of the creative journey is sharing your work with the world. What will they think? The "performance syndrome" from our years in school follows us throughout life—from the classroom to the office to the internet. If I release this song, post this poem, publish this writing, advance this idea…I may only get two likes and lots of negative comments. Or everyone in the meeting or the office will remain silent.

Reprogramming is needed to give us the confidence to transition from a terrifying point to a terrific point. It thus means you will need to define what your picture of success looks like. This picture should be more intrinsic than extrinsic. You want to be proud of your work and feel that it represents what you have to offer.

❧

What Are Default Settings?

Our decision-biases drive us into a state of autopilot, which defines our responses to situations, opportunities and challenges. This default setting does not lend itself to deviations and creative thinking, as it is characterized by routine/ritualistic thought processes suited well for "mass production." This means that if you think and act like everyone else, you will get what everybody else gets—average output.

Our default settings are usually informed by our past experiences, values, and beliefs and often by some form of minor or major trauma. It is important to identify what are the sources of our default settings. Become more alert to your life's journey, past and present, and to the stage you are at currently. How do you respond to your creative intuition, your creative ideas? Do you push them away? Do you get excited about developing your ideas? Do you immediately start telling everyone you come in contact with? How, when, and where do you express your creativity?

And what about your comfort zone? Your comfort zone is not a state you have just found yourself in. It is a place that has been developed over time, based on your default settings, in order to provide you with a place of safety, a place where you have control. But it can also block your creativity. Your comfort zone may be set up in a way that your creativity is stifled or kind of stuck in a corner.

In that case, it could be time to blow off the lid!

❧

Stepping Out of Your Comfort Zone

In his paper, "From Comfort Zone to Performance Management," Alasdair White, a British management theorist, defines one's comfort zone as "a behavioral state within which a person operates in an anxiety-neutral condition, using a limited set of behaviors to deliver a steady level of performance, usually without a sense of risk."

Evaluating your comfort zone is a critical step toward promoting your creative genius and improving your life. Caution is needed when stepping out of your comfort zone to ensure that you are actually enhancing your creativity rather than just executing a mindless activity. Stepping out of your comfort zone and going "against the grain" may attract a label such as that of being a rebel, and that may be okay with you or not. Don't allow your journey beyond your comfort zone to be a box-ticking exercise. As you move away from conformity, don't let your actions lead you to a reckless state. Let your rebellion be responsible. Understand that you are simply making conscientious decisions to live more intentionally.

I didn't quit my job because I wasn't getting along with my boss but because I wanted to be able to explore my creative ideas and to enjoy the freedom of not being limited to a job function or department. You don't need to justify your motives to those around you, but you do need to be clear about your motives. Have that conversation with yourself.

The natural tendencies in the comfort zone are not all bad. When an artist wants to draw a flower petal, they have to pay attention to the details of lines, contours, and color depths to replicate the flower on a canvas. However, if that artist naturally pays attention to details in his life, then he need not step out of his comfort zone. It is important to know when to step out of your comfort zone and when not to.

Why Step Out of Your Comfort Zone?

You don't step out of your comfort zone to be creative; you step out of your comfort zone to push your boundaries and foster an environment where you can become more creative.

1. **Growth and change.**

   It is insane to do the same things over and over and expect different results. Growth only exists where there is change and progress. Stepping outside your comfort zone means identifying areas that need to be developed. If you have always been a shy person, then you will always choose situations that allow you to disappear. However, outside your comfort zone is where you will develop your people skills by doing things such as group presentations and other activities, unlocking a part of yourself that seemed unreachable before. Choose to let go of your hold on "safe" situations and choose to move forward towards growth.

   Creativity requires that you become comfortable with being uncomfortable. When you get used to being uncomfortable, then you will be able to think about and challenge your current situation. Mastering the art of being uncomfortable and always looking for new challenges is a part of creative growth. There must, however, be a method to your madness, and this is why it's important to craft your creativity.

   Putting yourself in unfamiliar territory forces you to learn new skills and to develop various aspects of your life, which then leads you to new opportunities. Take a look at who you are now and contrast that with who you were five to 10 years ago. What's different about you today? What are you doing now that you once thought you would never do? At times, circumstances force us to develop and to do things that we would not have imagined possible. I would certainly not have imagined being an author. I first started writing down my thoughts, then a newsletter, and now my first book—Blow the Lid Off. And I've started a movement for people who want to live crazy, creative lives.

2. **Learn to deal with failure. (Give yourself permission to fail.)**

Creativity comes with its share of failures, as what you imagine may not necessarily come out by stepping out of your comfort zone, you raise your anxiety and fear levels slightly above normal as you attempt to try new things. It's very likely you will experience moments of failure at first but then your mind goes to work to creatively find solutions. Of course, this is not automatic and it will require you to have an open mind by not being fixated on the point of failure but instead having the courage and drive to move past that failure point. Leverage your imagination and curiosity to create new solutions to old problems. *"After all, failure is delay, not defeat."* – **Dennis Waitely**

"Anything worth doing is worth doing poorly – until you can learn to do it well." – **Zig Ziglar**

3. **Develop confidence.**

Have you ever been surprised after conquering a challenge that seemed impossible at first? Then you perhaps oozed with confidence knowing that you overcame your fears, reservations, and doubts around that challenge. Confidence gives you that "proud of yourself" moment. It fuels your ability to take on more challenges and conquer them. This can only happen when you give up your sense of control, when you allow yourself to operate in unfamiliar territory and trust your instincts, knowledge, and creativity. This boost in confidence, when channeled toward your creative process, allows you to continually push the boundaries of your imagination—despite the status quo. In the aforementioned Adobe report, 22% of respondents said being creative made them more confident.

4. **Adaptability.**

Navigating the unknown path not only requires you to learn new skills, it also forces you to shift and adapt to this new environment. Raising your levels of curiosity and flexibility allow you to grasp how best to adjust. Thus, adapting is not merely coping; it is enabling you to tap into your intellect and see things from a different perspective, while embracing risk. The many disruptions in our world today mean that we need to be adaptable, which can in turn promote more creativity.

Despite being a frequent air traveler, I had a huge fear of heights. Over the years, I challenged myself by sitting at the window seats on the airplane, going to the top of high buildings and looking down, etc. These activities helped to diminish my fear of heights, but I still had moments when the fear would rush right back at me. I also noticed that despite it being a fear specific to heights, it also affected other aspects of my life. I decided that I needed to do something outside my comfort zone that would give me that big breakthrough, not only with heights but with other areas of my life. While on vacation and taking a swim in the ocean, I noticed people parachuting onto the beach. This activity had always been on my "bucket list" and as I swam I said, "One day." However, I decided to reframe, and I changed "one day" to "today!" I immediately got out of the water and walked down the beach to the registration desk where I signed up for a tandem jump.

As we boarded the small aircraft, my first shock was that it had no door, just an opening. As we climbed to our altitude of 12,000 feet, I didn't feel fear. That wasn't until we started moving toward the door opening and hanging our feet out of the aircraft.

But before I could let it all sink in, out we went—falling at a terminal speed of about 200km/h. I definitely felt the fear as we twirled and twisted before stabilizing. At first, I closed my eyes, but then I gathered the courage to open them and I saw the earth from a new perspective. The parachute deployed and I looked at the earth in amazement! Then we were cruising onto the white sandy beach. It was truly one of the most fantastic experiences of my life!

The boost of confidence from that activity has fueled me to be fearless in life! The activity was not directly about being creative, I suppose, but that step, or should I say jump, out of my comfort zone revealed endless possibilities to me.

Did it blow the lid off? Yes!

Every year since then, I strive to do a bucket list activity.

Stepping out of your comfort zone does not necessarily mean doing adventurous outdoor activities. It means venturing into the unknown and doing things that are different or challenging and that will spark your creativity. It means stepping into the unexplored and stretching your boundaries.

Today or tomorrow could be the start of a new journey for you. What beckons you? What excites you? What inspires you?

And you don't have to make this journey alone. If you want some support, sign up on my website—and I can support you through the process.

Takeaways

Default settings provide a safe and familiar environment but they can stifle our creativity. Our comfort zone can be our prison.

Activities that take you out of your comfort zone may be scary, or even terrifying, but they can activate your creativity, supply you with insights, and help you discover parts of yourself that you didn't know existed, which means you can pursue achievements and adventures that otherwise would not have occurred to you.

I can promise you that once you move from a terrifying to a terrific place, you will not remain there. You will face more terrifying moments, as each stage of your journey challenges your comfort zone.

When you feel the fear or uncertainty of change, remember that the only constant in life is change. Use change to grow, to learn about yourself, to acquire new skills and abilities, and to live your creative, crazy life. While risk and fear are inherently present when you are stepping out and stretching your comfort zone, confidence and courage make it possible.

As Brené Brown stated, "We can choose courage or we can choose comfort, but we can't have both."

NOTES

_____

_____

_____

_____

_____

_____

_____

_____

_____

_____

_____

_____

_____

_____

_____

_____

_____

CHAPTER 4

Your Creativity
The Message of Your Itching Creative Gene

*"Every child is an artist. The problem is staying an artist when you grow up." – **Pablo Picasso***

Pablo Picasso was born in October 1881 in Spain. He is one of the greatest artists who ever lived. Picasso stood out for his technical mastery of painting and also because he was radical in his approach. His art journey was characterized by various periods, drawing inspiration from all his surroundings. Picasso showed the world that there was another dimension to an object, and he unapologetically rethought the traditional rules of painting.

By so doing, he cocreated the art of Cubism. [24]Cubism, a highly influential visual arts style of the twentieth century, was created principally by artists Picasso and George Braque in Paris between 1907 and 1914. The Cubist style emphasized the flat, two-dimensional surface of the picture plane, rejecting the traditional techniques of perspective, foreshortening, modelling, and chiaroscuro, and refuting the time-honored theories that art should imitate nature. Cubist painters were not bound to copying form, texture, color, and space; instead, they presented a new reality in paintings that depicted radically fragmented objects.

---

[24] The Editors of Encyclopaedia Britannica, "Cubism," *Encyclopaedia Britannica, Inc.*, June 20, 2019. https://www.britannica.com/art/Cubism.

Picasso was destined for greatness from an early age. Picasso recalled, "When I was a child, my mother said to me, 'If you become a soldier, you'll be a general. If you become a monk, you'll end up as the pope.`` Instead, I became a painter and I ended up as *Picasso.*"

Picasso's early education didn't reflect his promise—his grades were lackluster. "For being a bad student, I was banished to the "calaboose," a bare cell with whitewashed walls and a bench to sit on," he later remembered. "I liked it there, because I took along a sketch pad and drew incessantly...I could have stayed there forever, drawing without stopping."

☙

Purpose

The journey of creativity is a journey of self-discovery and self-development. Aligning your creative awakening with your life's mission will allow you to fully realize your creative genius by factoring in your uniqueness and setting the parameters that define your success. You thus move to a state of affirmation where your creative genius is intertwined with your life's mission. Therefore, you build resistance to the missiles of admonition coming from those who believe you should retreat to the safety of conformity. The affirmation of the creative journey is not dependent upon the acceptance of your ideas by others; it is dependent upon you affirming and embracing your inner creative child.

Often, we ask how to unleash our creativity, how to become more creative, or how to inspire creativity. Yes, we will get some great tips and advice, but they won't necessarily be the answers that align with our life. For example, if I want to lose weight, I can Google endless nutritional and exercise guides to get me to my goals, but none of these will factor in my individual uniqueness.

I busted my knee as a teenager playing football [soccer], so when I wanted to lose weight, I had to make sure this was factored into my plans.

What factors do you need to consider that will help you unleash your creativity? The pressure exerted by the lid that suppresses our creative gene will differ greatly from one person to the next.

Blowing the lid off is very much an individual task that will be very different for each person.

What is your uniqueness?

Do you know your purpose in life?

What is your life's mission?

There should be a deep and obvious connection between your creative goals and your personal mission statement. The creative process can be unstructured and cloudy at times, so knowing your mission helps you to navigate this unfamiliar terrain. Your mission is your compass, not your map. A map can't evolve according to changes in the environment. A compass, on the other hand, always points you to your mission—your true north. During your creative journey, you may find yourself totally off track, but your mission will set you back on course.

Before discovering my mission, I was a salesman, an accountant, an IT guy, and I even worked in procurement. Throughout these experiences, one theme was constant: that of being a pioneer, as in each instance, I would be the first person in that specific role.

Recruiters would tell me that my career lacked focus. I also believed I was just wandering in the darkness—until I looked at my compass. Since then, I have never been lost, even when I decided to write this maiden book.

Developing your creative thinking skills can be a powerful way to prompt new ideas, yet being creative often feels chaotic, uncomfortable, and unproductive. This is why defining your mission can keep you focused on your why. Your creativity is not something to be achieved or to be attained; it is a deep yearning that needs to be satisfied, a dimmed light that needs to be illuminated.

"Participating in creativity unlocks knowledge about oneself, others, and the world around them, providing an immense benefit to even those who do not consider themselves creative."[25]

ဆ

Not Your Mission

We can first look at what your mission is *not:*

1. Your career. Your career is just a means through which you achieve your mission. If you are a lawyer, you could be a lawyer whose mission is to help prevent marginalized widows from being taken advantage of, and you can do it with sympathy, compassion, and humor.

2. A title. Your mission is not about achieving a particular title or position, such as achieving a master's degree or a PhD. However, these accolades can sometimes be a tool to help you achieve your mission.

3. Your skills. You may be highly skilled at something but that doesn't mean it's your mission.

4. Contentment. Your mission is not merely to survive; it is not just about being able to work, pay the bills, and provide for your family.

5. Being a faithful spouse or a good neighbor. While these are great things to be, they are more like responsibilities, not a mission.

[25] Silvia, Paul & Beaty, Roger & Nusbaum, Emily & Eddington, Kari & Levin-Aspenson, Holly & Kwapil, Thomas. (2014). "Everyday Creativity in Daily Life: An Experience-Sampling Study of 'Little c' Creativity." Psychology of Aesthetics Creativity and the Arts. 8. 10.1037/a0035722.

"Never permit a dichotomy to rule your life, a dichotomy in which you hate what you do so you can have pleasure in your spare time. Look for a situation in which your work will give you as much happiness as your spare time." – **Pablo Picasso**

Your Mission (Who Needs Your Light?)

Use the following P-guide matrix to help you structure your thoughts around your mission:

1. *Passion & Personality:* What are you passionate about? Discovering your passion revolves around what fuels you or what excites you. What can you do over and over again without even thinking about it? It is typically something that you do without much effort; it comes naturally. It could be a cause you feel deeply about or something that you can't stop thinking about. Your passion is something that you envision can be approached in different ways— something you can do differently and with your own flavor.

    Even throughout your career, there are things that may or may not have been in your job description but that you would gladly do and help others to do the same. Look back at your life and you may notice a pattern emerging. Also, your passion is typically something that you give away easily and don't expect to be paid for it. At lunch, meetings, conferences, or family gatherings, you are just known for this and you have received compliments about it but perhaps you have never paid much attention to it.

    "Passion is one great force that unleashes creativity, because if you're passionate about something, then you're more willing to take risks." – **Yo-Yo Ma**

2. *People with Problems:* Your mission is linked to solving a specific problem, a problem that is close to you, that is within your domain. There are so many problems that we face on a daily basis and that we may help people with, but there is

a specific problem that you identify with and that you are "passionate" about. It's an area in which you provide the solution by letting your light shine. I am passionate about helping people realize the value of their uniqueness through activating their suppressed creative gene. (This is not exactly how my mission is stated but just another way of looking at it for this example.) The problem that is close to me is a problem I went through myself. One of my heroes, Nelson Mandela, was fighting to solve the ugly problem of apartheid. Why was this problem close to him? Mandela interacted with people from a wide variety of backgrounds and beliefs. He experienced racism firsthand and he saw how it was affecting so many black South Africans. He opened the first black law firm in South Africa, along with his friend Oliver Tambo. His law profession was not his mission; rather, he used the skills acquired through practicing law to help black South Africans to be properly represented, and at an affordable rate, in a court of law. (Existing law firms were charging extremely high rates to represent their black clients in court.) Then Mandela honed his skills to enter politics—not to get a position but to further his mission. The following is part of his famous "Speech from the Dock:"

"I have fought against white domination, and I have fought against black domination. I have cherished the ideal of a democratic and free society in which all persons live together in harmony and with equal opportunities. It is an ideal which I hope to live for and to achieve. But if needs be, it is an ideal for which I am prepared to die."

On 8 June 2013, in an article titled "Nelson Mandela's life and times," the BBC commentator stated, "His charisma, self-deprecating sense of humor, and lack of bitterness over his harsh treatment, as well as his amazing life story, partly explain his extraordinary global appeal."

Mandela knew what he was passionate about and he sought to solve the issue by being himself and personifying what he believed in. Because the only person that you will really be good at being is yourself! Your passion and your creativity cannot be outsourced. Own it, use it, and reveal it.

*"Creativity is a spark. It can be excruciating when we're rubbing two rocks together and getting nothing. And it can be intensely satisfying when the flame catches and a new idea sweeps around the world." – **Jonah Lehrer***

❧

What Do the Signs Say?

Go through each sign below and think of when it is most evident in your life. What are the circumstances, what are you doing, what is your role, where are you, etc.? By doing so, you get to dig deeper to discover the true message of your creative gene and how it aligns with your life's mission.

1. **You like problem solving.**

   You like solving problems and you are ready to accept the challenge even when you may not be sure how the problem could be solved. You get energized because looking for a solution gives you an opportunity to use your imagination—and yes, of course, your creativity. Alternatively, perhaps you have not yet realized your attraction to problem solving, but somehow, people keep coming to you for advice on how to handle various problems. At times, you just do your best and help out, but the solution you provide is really appreciated by the other person(s)—when to you it either didn't seem that difficult or you weren't even sure if it would work.

2. **You ask many questions.**

    You just somehow cannot stop yourself from seeking to un-
    derstand the origin of various things, behaviors, or people.
    And it is difficult for you to accept that things should always
    remain the way they are. You tend to inquire instead of just
    accepting, and your inquisitive tendencies are evident. You
    sit and tell yourself that something could have been done
    differently, not from a position of condemnation of anyone
    but from a position that there is a better way.

3. **You don't quite fit in.**

    Yes, you are liked and appreciated, but at the end of the day
    you seem to stick out in the crowd. Remember that most
    people desire to fit in and are willing to accept things the
    way they are but you can't really do that. You are natural-
    ly inquisitive and curious and creative. You, therefore, may
    find it hard to be your true self with others, or at least with
    some folks, because you can predict that they won't quite
    "get" you.

4. **You are highly adaptable.**

    This might seem contrary to point number three but you
    are able to adjust and blend into various groups, crowds, or
    gatherings if that is what you desire to do. You can converse
    happily with the security guard or the waiter or the janitor
    and then go straight to the CEO's office without having to
    think much about it.

5. **You have a problem with authority.**

    Your inquisitive mind leads to clashes with those in au-
    thority. This is because your seemingly default setting is to
    question before following. And this type of questioning is
    not asking how high to jump but more like, "Why are we

jumping?" or "Is this the best way to achieve the desired result?" or "What technique should we use to jump?" etc. At times, you may even be admonished. And you may sometimes be seen as someone who does not respect authority or who tends to second guess instructions. When your life's mission is known, then your creative questioning may be better understood.

There are other signs that might be unique to you, and you should be observant and take note of the situation, circumstances, and messaging, which, in essence, is referred to as autobiographical planning. This is where you look back at your life and use self-reflection to take note of the highs and lows, victories and failures, and you build a personal future-focused narrative. Also, there are soft skills that usually accompany creativity, so examine this aspect in light of things like courage, boldness, playfulness, and adventure.

*"Creativity is a combinatorial force: it's our ability to tap into our 'inner' pool of resources — knowledge, insight, information, inspiration and all the fragments populating our minds — that we've accumulated over the years just by being present and alive and awake to the world and to combine them in extraordinary new ways." – **Maria Popova, Brain Pickings***

Share with us your creativity affirmations online using the hashtag #BlowTheLidOff.

⁓

Mission Sent

One other thing that greatly helped me learn more about myself and my mission was finding out more about where I came from. I am not talking about learning my ancestry and meeting strangers from halfway around the world. Certainly not! I am talking about my creation. I don't know your spiritual persuasions, but I am a firm believer in the creation account of mankind. I believe I was created by an all-powerful God in his image and likeness. In his image and likeness, not so much that he has hands and feet and ears, but that I possess an element of creative power. Creative power through my creative gene to invent, to create new perspectives based on my uniqueness. This I do not for my own reward or glory but to lift Him up as the source of power.

I believe that we have all been given our unique special talents, and degree of creativity, to make an impact on humanity; that our time and presence here on earth must be productive, not only for those we interact with but also for those who will come after us. In Jeremiah, chapter 1:5, the Lord tells Jeremiah, "Before I formed you in the womb, I knew you before you were born, I set you apart…"

Marianne Williamson, an American spiritual leader, politician, activist, and author of 13 books states,

> *"Our deepest fear is not that we are inadequate. Our deepest fear is that we are powerful beyond measure. It is our light, not our darkness, that most frightens us. We ask ourselves: Who am I to be brilliant, gorgeous, talented, fabulous? Actually, who are you not to be? You are a child of God. Your playing small does not serve the world. There is nothing enlightened about shrinking so that other people won't feel insecure around you. We are all meant to shine as children do. We were born to make manifest the glory of God that is within us. It's not just in some of us; it's in everyone. And as we let our own light shine, we unconsciously give other people permission to do the same. As we are liberated from our own fear, our presence automatically liberates others."*

My purpose is to help to contribute to a generation of people who will live creative lives with confidence and joy.

You may have started this chapter clueless about your mission and perhaps even doubting that you are special—well, I want to let you know that you are indeed special, unique, and valued. And this is why I wrote this book for you—embrace it and reflect upon it so you can unleash the person you are meant to be. Someone whose life matters to so many people because of your uniqueness to help solve a problem that is dear to you and to so many others. I recommend that you reach out to our all-powerful Creator for revelations and insights regarding who you are meant to be. When you discover yourself, be bold, be strong, and be unwavering.

*"In the same way, let your light so shine before men that they may see your good deeds and glorify your Father in heaven." – **Matthew 5:16***

Takeaways

The potent message of your creative gene is the message of your mission!

The discovery of creativity brings affirmation regarding your uniqueness. Your life's mission is a journey that can only be taken by you. Aligning your mission with your creative journey strengthens your resolve to blow the lid off and express your creativity without reservation.

Your life experiences are rich with lessons and principles which, when examined, will reveal a message. Your message will align perfectly with your mission and give you a destiny with purpose. The journey of your life has been filled with many triggers that affect your creative gene. When your mission interacts with your creative gene, you have the overwhelming feeling of purpose and destiny and that brings with it happiness, joy, and confidence.

NOTES

CHAPTER 5

Blown Lid
Breaking New Ground

> *"It took the madmen of yesterday for us to be able to act with extreme clarity today. I want to be one of those madmen. We must dare to invent the future."*
> **– Thomas Sankara**

Have you ever observed a big truck making a turn around a corner?

One of the first things they do is make an announcement! They signal with their loud air horn blast —*Bwwooooooppp!*

When I was a young boy, I thought the signaling was to draw our attention to it. I would just stand there and observe this huge vehicle make its daring turn. As I grew older, I discovered that the signaling was more to warn other road users and even pedestrians to watch out, as there could be possible danger if one did not pay attention. Oh, the excitement of a young boy in observing the impressive maneuver of that large transporter!

This chapter is largely going to be action-oriented, journeying from ideation to implementation, and like the truck, I want you to make that turn, that shift in your life, and BLOW the lid off!

The first stage of the implementation of your creative idea is revelation. It's realizing that you are going to turn those adventurous ideas into reality!

_ℰℐ_

Squeeze Your Air Horn!

One author writes, "Like a plant constrained in the same pot, our roots become bound and twisted. Over time we're unable to be fully nourished. We can't grow beyond the limits of our environment."

I want you to be able to grow beyond the limits of your environment! Stop managing your life and start _creating_ it. _Managing_ your life does not consider new possibilities; it focuses on getting by with what you have. _Creating_ your life means breaking the flowerpot and extending your roots to wherever they need to go. You have decided that today will be the first day of your new life. Cement your decision by taking action now!

So here is how we are going to take action:

Transfer to paper:

I want you to use the space provided below and write down three of your craziest creative ideas. These may be ideas you have had in your mind for a long time or maybe they are new. In any case, write them down.

[26]"Words are simply symbols for thoughts and ideas. Every time you write or say a word, you evoke a vision in your mind." At this point, I don't want you to worry about the how. I don't want you to worry about the when. I don't want you to worry about the possibility or practicability. I just want you to evoke the vision in your mind—to activate your creative gene.

Be a child again, full of imagination. Don't judge your ideas— just write them down. This is why you are reading this book, because the time is now.

---

[26] Newberry, Tommy. _Success Is Not an Accident: Change Your Choices; Change Your Life._ Illinois: Tyndale House Publishers, 2007.

Feel free to be descriptive, but avoid getting into granular details. We are not setting goals here; we are just writing down ideas.

Crazy Ideas:

1. _____

_____

_____

_____

2. _____

_____

_____

_____

3. _____

_____

_____

_____

How did that activity make you feel?

Well I have even better news for you. I want you to dig deeper. I want you to totally let your creative gene lead your thinking. Your three crazy ideas above might still be restrictive, simply because of the strength of the logical side of your brain. Now I want you to write down two more crazy, creative ideas. But this time, I want these two ideas to be absolutely insane. These two ideas should represent your super-stretched imagination. Again, don't worry about timelines and whether or not your ideas are achievable. Just write. Don't doubt yourself.

Crazier Ideas:

1. _____

_____

_____

_____

2. _____

_____

_____

_____

Paint your picture:

This is going to be a visualization exercise through painting. Your canvas is your future and you are the painter. Following the above activity, your creative gene should be triggered; its manifestation on paper cements its uniqueness and value.

Schedule quiet, reflective time to do this activity. Choose a time and environment when your creative juices will flow.

The picture you paint is one that represents your creative life as you imagine it. Simply think about and imagine what the world will be like when you achieve your ultimate creative ideas. Think of this picture as your calling card. Saturate your work with emotion; fuse your five senses and let that guide your use of color.

Don't think of how your life or world is right now; manifest what you have in your imagination. Again, don't worry about the practicality or possibility; remove those limitations and develop the picture that's in your imagination.

Let your painting be your base. Then feel free to build on it and develop it by making use of technology to further illustrate your picture—but only after you have done the painting. If you are musically inclined, why not write a melody that accompanies your painting or write a poem that enhances it. Have fun!

Okay. Congratulations! I hope you love what you created!

But guess what?

You still have not yet squeezed your air horn! What you have done so far is simply load your truck with cargo. Now we are confident that we have precious cargo onboard and we want to make a big turn towards our new creative life. So how do we squeeze the horn? By an announcement! A confident declaration!

We live in a social digital world and it's only getting more social and more digital. So get your thumbs ready. I want you to go to social media and tell the world that…

"Today is the start of living my crazy, creative life!"

Of course, you don't need to use those exact words; that would be boring and lacking in originality. What's more, some of you might choose to create a video, or design a poster, or…The only rules are:

Be yourself—your true self, your new creative self.

Use the following hashtag so I can follow along and we can start this movement and encourage each other: #BlowTheLidOff.

Join our community to receive more support by signing up at https://mailchi.mp/ce4a0dc12e5d/blowthelidoff.

I can't wait to "hear" your air horn blasting all across the world!

Congratulations!!!!

You have now observed the principle of Speed of Implementation. This principle simply states that the quicker you implement something new that you've heard or seen, the more likely it's going to be ingrained in your memory. You have turned an idea into action. Hey, don't take this for granted; you have just made a gigantic step and you should celebrate it!

☙

Turn Your Head

The next thing that a truck driver does is turn the head of the truck in the desired direction. This happens even while the truck is stationary. The most critical step towards progress and success is to shift your focus! Your life will only change if you precede it with a choice—a choice to accept that where you are now is not where you belong. Then make the choice to change your direction. Let your choice to change help you to turn your challenges into opportunities and to change the direction of your life. Your actions cannot be wiser than your thinking, and your thinking can be no wiser than your understanding.

The body of the truck cannot go where the head is not focused. So too in our lives, you have to focus intently on where you want to go. That is why we did the air horn exercise above, and if you haven't done it, I encourage you to pause and to go back and get it done.

Tony Robbins stated, "Where focus goes, energy flows." Your energy is interlinked with your creativity. Remember that this is a journey, not a race. When you think that you are not making progress, remember the truck. The truck will not be able to negotiate the turn without first making some minor adjustments. It may even come to a standstill first, but there is also progress in stillness. Learn not to measure progress only by movement.

Takeaways (New Ground)

Again, congratulations to you for blowing the lid off! You have now broken new ground. Breaking new ground is an exhilarating time; it sets the stage for new possibilities. However, this is where the work must begin. The truck example requires a combination of fuel, power, and skill to successfully maneuver the turn—just as construction projects break new ground and the work of excavation provides the setting for the foundation of the structure.

I want to challenge you to be a "mad man," as General Thomas Sankara refers to in our opening quotation. Take a look at the ideas you wrote down in this chapter. If these ideas were implemented, would they make a positive impact on people's lives? Are they just ideas for yourself, or are they ideas that can make a noticeable difference in the life of others? Are they ideas that could invent the future?

Fuse your child-like creative freedom with your passion to harness your creativity. Look again at your mission. Now that you have written down your crazy ideas, how do they compare to the thoughts you have so far about your mission? Use these ideas to help you get further clarity on your mission. Schedule time to deeply think through what we have covered so far, writing down any questions you may have, and see if they will be answered as we go along.

This concludes the first part of this book. In the second part, we will look at establishing the support structures for living a creative life. We will get more practical in our approach—shifting more toward left-brain approaches to creativity.

NOTES

Part Two

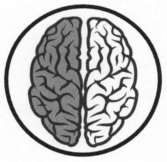

CHAPTER 6

Living It!
It's Not a Diet; It's a Lifestyle!

> *"I'm not very creative" doesn't work. There's no such thing as creative people and noncreative people. There are only people who use their creativity and people who don't. Unused creativity doesn't just disappear. It lives within us until it's expressed, neglected to death, or suffocated by resentment and fear.* — **Brené Brown**

Welcome to the second part of *Blow the Lid Off* where you will learn how to *Craft Your Creativity.*

In this part, we will focus more on practical approaches regarding how to live creatively by tapping into our left-brain circuit and discovering how to craft those *crazy* ideas. This is where the rubber meets the road, where we will see how our new creative life can me maintained as we interact with the world around us.

Your new thought process must ensure that you see creativity not just as an episode or activity to be scheduled like art class but as a lifestyle—*your* lifestyle!

No Dieting

In my life, I draw a lot of lessons from health. I am always trying to improve my mental health by ensuring that I have a strategy to deal with stress and that my thoughts are positive and affirmative. Physically, I like to keep moving and challenging my body to break new limits. Emotionally, I strive to better understand my response mechanisms and to use my emotions as data points to help me better respond to situations and to people. Nutritionally, I ensure that I educate myself on my caloric requirements based on my goals and that I don't use a one-size-fits-all approach. Balancing my macro and micro nutrients gives me the latitude to be flexible in my consumption. I don't do all this as a short-term goal; I do this because it aligns with my principles and goals. Therefore, I don't see this practice as a burden.

When someone diets, they go through a period of restrictions on foods that are seen to be unhealthy or fattening. Typically, there is an obsession with *"How long do I have to do this?"* or *"How long will it take to get results?"* Although it is good to set targets and have expectations, such questions reveal the intention of a myopic journey. The focus is singular in nature and perhaps that is why weight gain recurs later on.

A lifestyle is a reflection of *yourself* and how you wish to live and to be perceived. Improving your creative consciousness will guide you to live a more empowered life. This allows you to take a creative approach to *every* aspect of your life—daily living, making changes, overcoming fears and insecurities, interacting with others, approaching and solving problems, and your general perception of life. You blow the lid off, and you refuse to be constrained or held back.

In Abraham Maslow's hierarchy of needs, the path to self-actualization includes the pursuit of creativity, i.e., a self-actualized person is a creative person. He presents the characteristic of creativity as a universal trait that is present in everyone.

Maslow's position is not that every self-actualized person is an artist, or a musician, or a writer but that these types of creative activities are just one expression of a healthy personality.

"My feeling is that the concept of creativeness and the concept of the healthy, self-actualizing, fully human person seem to be coming closer

and closer together, and may perhaps turn out to be the same thing."
— *Abraham Maslow*

Creativity in Everything You Do

Creativity is not mutually exclusive to the arts, or sciences, or sports, or as in my case finance and accounting. Instead, creativity is vital to the improvement and success of these disciplines.

Inventor and physicist Albert Einstein was a creative, and he fused his creativity into his groundbreaking discoveries. It has been noted that most of his groundbreaking work was a result of his creative thinking more than his underlying technical knowledge of the subject matter. He played the piano and violin, which he would do to refocus his efforts on his scientific work. Self-declaring his dependency on creativity, Einstein stated, "I am enough of an artist to draw freely upon my imagination. Imagination is more important than knowledge. Knowledge is limited. Imagination encircles the world."

As he discovered more and achieved groundbreaking results, he became more convinced. He believed more in intuition and inspiration than the absorption of absolute knowledge, and he promoted this position in his writings.

"The true sign of intelligence is not knowledge but imagination."
— *Albert Einstein*

He recorded in his autobiographical notes that he never thought in logical symbols or mathematical equations but in images, feelings, and even musical architectures. He has shown us that scholarly creativity produces a life of discovery and achievement, and he notes that the greatest scientists are artists as well.

David W. Galenson and Bruce A. Weinberg conducted a study along these lines. The study, titled *Creative Careers: The Life Cycles of Nobel Laureates in Economics*, concludes that what they discovered is not limited to economics but "could apply to creativity generally."

They stated, "In view of the practical importance of the life cycle of scholarly creativity, it is surprising that it has received little systematic study, and virtually none by economists. This may be because many academics think they already understand it. Many economists, for example, appear to believe creativity is the particular domain of the young."

You Have Not Missed Your Chance to Impact the World!

Continuing to dispel the myth that creativity is only for a select few, we see that it is not too late to reignite your "five-year-old creative genius." You can move from a *mini-c* creative level to a *Big-C* creative level by learning how to bring out your creativity using both your right- and left-brain hemispheres.

Your imagination, your creativity, and your crazy ideas can have an impact, solve problems, and earn you money. Even if you didn't complete high school or attend a university, you can still have amazing, creative ideas. Also, working in a traditional noncreative career does not prevent you from using your creativity to have an impact within your sphere of influence. You can create outstanding results and productivity.

As for age, if you are in your forties, fifties, sixties, seventies, or beyond, don't think that your best years are behind you and that you are too old to be creative. As you can see in the chart below, Benjamin Franklin invented bifocal glasses when he was 78. On the other hand, Louis Braille invented the Braille system when he was 15.

Some of the greatest inventors were not exclusively into inventing nor were they working in a creative field. And they were not limited by their age.

Here is a list of famous inventors who are examples of harnessing their creative and innovative ideas to change the world.

Name	Profession	Age	Invention
Benjamin Franklin	• Postmaster of Philadelphia • Founding Father • Ambassador to France	1. 78 2. 46	1. Bifocal glasses 2. Lightning rod
John Deere	• Blacksmith	33	World's first tractor
Johannes Gutenberg	• Goldsmith	44	First printing press
Louis Braille	• Teacher	15	Invented Braille system
Marie Curie	• Governess	31	• Discovered radioactivity • Only person to win two Nobel Peace Prizes

There are lots of examples of artists who were also inventors, including Leonardo da Vinci and Michelangelo. They both contributed to fields other than art, including engineering and science—da Vinci's creative expression spanned across the spectrum of human endeavor, including inventing the helicopter, the parachute, the submarine, etc. Being a pioneer in the study of light, he is also credited with the invention of the camera obscura, upon which the principle of modern photography is based. And he was the first European to paint landscapes, shifting the focus from objects to patterns.

Samuel Morse was an artist who invented Morse code. He is also famous for notable portraits of John Adams and James Monroe.

Robert Fulton went from painting miniatures to building submarines. And he is best known for the creation of the first commercial steamboat.

A typist named Bette Nesmith Graham loved painting when she was not at the office. Her artistic passions led her to develop a quick-drying paint that later became liquid paper—the brand famous for correction fluids like white-out, as well as correction pens and correction tape.

Renowned actress Hedy Lamarr created and patented what she and her partners referred to as a "Secret Communication System." Her patent is widely used in wireless internet transmission and it became integral to securing military communications and mobile phone technology.

As a teenager, I loved reading the encyclopedia and trying out most of the experiments. Then my curiosity regarding innovative endeavors continually led me to the work being done by MIT (Massachusetts Institute of Technology). I wanted to attend MIT and have a shot at making groundbreaking discoveries, and I pictured myself studying electrical engineering. I then began to learn about the state of Massachusetts as I pictured my new living place, and I got as far as meeting a recruiter and mapping out my journey. With the excitement of attending MIT, I decided to visit my cousin who was studying Nano Engineering at Manchester University. As he showed me around the university, my desire to go to MIT grew stronger. Well, life happened, and I didn't manage to attend MIT. I would later decide to stay in my lane and attend a local university and study accounting.

Then in 2004, two researchers at the University of Manchester—Professor Andre Geim and Professor Kostya Novoselov—started something called "Friday night experiments"—sessions where they would try out experimental science that wasn't necessarily linked to their day jobs. Despite a 15-year gap in their ages, the two researchers enjoyed trying out new things together. Then one night, while messing around with flakes of graphite, the curiosity to investigate its electrical properties led them to use sticky tape to make thinner flakes. After repeatedly peeling off layers, they got down to the layer where it was only one atom thick—thus discovering graphene.

Graphene is considered to be the wonder material; it is 100 times stronger than steel by weight and is the thinnest and strongest substance known to man. It is the best conductor of heat, and its possible uses include foldable electronics and DNA sequencing. Its application is widespread, including foldable smartphones and it may replace the iconic Lithium mobile battery.

Their groundbreaking experiment led them to be jointly awarded the Nobel Prize in physics in 2010 for their two-dimensional material. The Nobel committee highlighted the playful approach of the two researchers. "A playful idea is perfect to start things, but then you need really good scientific intuition that your playful experiment will lead to something, or it will stay as a joke forever," Novoselov stated.

What are your creative ideas?

The blowing-the-lid-off exercise in the previous chapter is meant to unearth some of those crazy ideas of yours. If you haven't done it yet, this is the next best time for you to get it done. Take some time to think it through, but as I advised above, don't take too much time. Doing it now will help to focus your reading of the rest of the book to be more personalized.

If you were able to live differently and do things differently, what would you be doing? Would you remove yourself from behind your desk and computer screen and start a daycare or school to impact the lives of children? Would you move from the office and explore your comedic or poetic skills? What would you like to venture into? What have you always wondered about or desired to explore and do? Picture yourself living more creatively!

Build the road to get you there by carving out your own path.

Get those crazy ideas out of your head and out into the world.

☙

Don't Ignore the Arts

A study by Michigan State University (MSU)[27] revealed that *participation in arts and crafts leads to innovation (and patents), and increases the odds of starting a business as an adult.* The team studied the university's honor students from 1990 to 1995 who majored in STEM subjects.

(STEM is a curriculum based on the idea of educating students in four specific disciplines—science, technology, engineering, and mathematics—in an interdisciplinary and applied approach.)

"The most interesting finding was the importance of sustained participation in those activities," said Rex LaMore, director of MSU's Center for Community and Economic Development. "If you started as a young child and continued in your adult years,

---

[27] Lamore, Rex & Root-Bernstein, Robert & Root-Bernstein, Michele & Schweitzer, John & Lawton, James & Roraback, Eileen & Peruski, Amber & VanDyke, Megan & Fernandez, Laleah. (2013). "Arts and Crafts Critical to Economic Innovation." Economic Development Quarterly. 27. 221-229. 10.1177/0891242413486186.

you're more likely to be an inventor, as measured by the number of patents generated, businesses formed, or articles published. And that was something we were surprised to discover."

Regardless of your current position in life, you can still spark and harness your creativity. Don't be limited to what you studied in school or what you have been exposed to. Use the arts to give you empowerment to live creatively. Explore outwards from your domain. A key component of creativity is cognitive flexibility, which is the ability to jump between different ideas. Gather data and information about your unique life experiences. But go further; consider new and different life experiences.

❧

Creativity Makes Everything Better. Start Here.

Interacting and appreciating creativity should be your stepping stone toward living a more creative life and producing high-impact, valuable solutions. If we consider the creative arts as the primary level of creativity and other nontraditional areas as secondary, then we can utilize the primary level to build up to the secondary level.

At the age of five, a child most often enjoys playing, dancing, music, and artistic activities. Can you relate to these experiences? And to trying your hand at almost anything because you approach it with an open mind?

The Brain and Creativity Institute at the University of South California conducted a two-year research study and discovered that children who are exposed to music education have better brain development and accelerated maturity of auditory processing than those who are not exposed. The study looked at six- and seven-year-olds over a two-year period.

A separate study that observed older adults (older than 40 years) who had received a moderate amount of music education (four to 14 years) found that the auditory systems in these adults did not experience the usual age-related declines related to sound recognition that is normally seen in adults. The study suggests, "It may be that early music instruction instills a fixed change in the central auditory system that is retained throughout life."

Just as with Einstein, there are many other successful creative people who have had some form of exposure to musical education. It's as if music opens up the pathways to creative thinking, improving the ability to connect what is seen and known to what does not yet exist—empowerment to make manifest the unseen. Microsoft cofounder Paul Allen played violin at an early age and then switched to the guitar in his teenage years. Playing instruments would be his escape from day-long programming, reenergizing him to be more creative. He said that music "reinforces your confidence in the ability to create."

Let's ensure that we expose our children to these creative activities even if they won't necessarily continue with them later on in life. Let's not allow music and the arts to be cancelled or reduced in our schools. Further, they need to be given *more* resources, including time, as they are *not* extracurricular activities; they are *core activities* for the human mind. True education must give equitable weighting to the sciences and the arts.

Creativity Requires Your Whole Brain

Another way to make creativity your lifestyle is to ensure that you involve your entire brain, i.e., leveraging your various learning styles. Apparently, the theory of left brain or right brain to distinguish our learning styles "lacks a basis in solid science, and is more of an urban myth."[28]

---

[28] Stephen M. Kosslyn, Ph.D. and G. Wayne Miller, "The Theory of Cognitive Modes," Psychology Today: October 2015.

The different sides (hemispheres) of our brain have different and specific functions, and they process data differently. Indeed, right-brain dominant folks are more creative and intuitive; while left-brain dominant folks are more logical, rational, and sequential.

The iconic creative and innovative people we looked at earlier in the chapter cannot be easily slotted into either of these categories. Clearly, they operate with both. Essentially, to be truly creative and to develop your creativity requires you to practice cognitive flexibility.

[29]Research by Prof. Klaus Hoppe shows this interhemispheric exchange necessary for creative functioning.

Also, it is known that the *corpus callosum* transfers information between the two hemispheres for activities, such as coordination and balancing.

Ned Herman developed the Whole Brain® Thinking model, which breaks the brain down into *four* quadrants—two in each hemisphere. This model shows that thinking through and using all four quadrants will lead to improved performance and output. It means moving away from operating only out of your dominant quadrant and moving toward operating out of all four. The use of cognitive flexibility then greatly increases and develops your creative genius.

Finally, let your creative lifestyle also incorporate time to just sit and relax. Sit by the ocean and listen to the waves, go for a hike, look at a sunset or sunrise, gaze at a piece of art, and see if you get the story. Reduce your screen time, avoid digital dementia, and open your eyes to your environment.

---

[29] Klaus D. Hoppe & Neville L. Kyle, "Dual brain, creativity, and health," Creativity Research Journal, 3:2, (1990) 150-157, DOI: 10.1080/10400419009534348.

❧

Let your life fuel your creativity

While a picture can be worth a thousand words, choose to look at fewer pictures and instead read 1,000 words and imagine what that picture looks like. Get used to slowing down so you can truly feel what you have experienced, and allow what you have captured through sensory means to synthesize in your brain.

I advocate travelling to expose one to different cultures and possibilities, particularly by immersing oneself at the local level. Move out of your comfort zone. Don't travel just for the sake of racking up air miles but to get a better understanding of other lifestyles and other cultures. This will help teach you how to develop an outsider's approach, which you can then apply to many situations and gain fresh new perspectives. St. Augustine stated, "…life is a book, and those who don't travel read only a page." Enjoy and embrace new sights, sounds, smells, and feelings to spark your creativity.

From a cognitive perspective, creativity scholars suggest that multicultural experiences have a positive influence on creative potential for four different reasons: (a) They allow individuals to have exposure to a wider variety of concepts and ideas; (b) They destabilize routinized thinking; (c) They increase one's psychological readiness to accept and use different concepts and ideas; and (d) They encourage the synthesis of incompatible ideas and concepts coming from different cultures.[30] [31]

A group of researchers in a submitted study to Proceedings of

---

[30] Leung, A. K., Maddux, W. W., Galinksy, A. D., & Chiu, C.-Y. (2008). "Multicultural experience enhances creativity." American Psychologist, 63(3), 169–181. DOI:10.1037/0003-066X.63.3.169.

[31] Leung, A. K., & Chiu, C.-Y. (2010). "Multicultural experience, idea receptiveness, and creativity." Journal of Cross-Cultural Psychology, 41, 723–741. DOI:10.1177/0022022110361707.

the National Academy of Sciences (PNAS) sought to understand the brain function connectivity of a creative individual. "Using methods in network neuroscience, we modelled individual creative thinking ability as a function of variation in whole-brain functional connectivity. We identified a brain network associated with creative ability comprised of regions within default, salience, and executive systems—neural circuits that often work in opposition."

The *default mode* is engaged when you daydream and your mind simply wanders off, such as when folding laundry or on your daily commute. Your brain is at rest but directed to a particular goal or objective. This helps with idea generation. The *executive network* is activated when you are fully engaged in activities, such as learning and decision-making, thus helping with idea evaluation, while the *salience network* works like a regulator and facilitates dynamic transitions between default and executive systems. Interestingly, these three networks don't get activated at the same time. But the creative person is able to process insights and engage both default and executive networks simultaneously.

One of my favorite downtime activities is washing dishes. This is because it puts my mind on autopilot, and I find that quite a number of random things pop up and I try to make connections between them. Similar to ideas that pop up in the shower. Strangely, this activity is also beneficial when I am feeling stressed. Going for a walk and exercising also does wonders for my creative process, as it helps to clear my mind—sort of like a "delete all operations" exercise, giving me a clean sheet approach to my thoughts.

Disrupt Your Patterns

Routines are great ways to ensure that we remain efficient. However, overreliance on routines can suppress our creativity. It then becomes a diet and not a lifestyle. In order to prime your creativity, you need to ensure it is present all day long by interrupting your patterns. It's insane to do the same things over and over and expect a different result, and here is where pattern interruption comes in. Pattern interruption allows you to redirect your thoughts and actions from being controlled by your unconscious mind to being controlled by your conscious mind, thus opening up new possibilities. Have you ever driven or walked to your home only to realize upon arrival that you can't recall the actual journey? We can perform routine activities such as daily commutes without even thinking about them. Another natural resistance to pattern interruption could be an "If it ain't broke, why fix it?" mindset.

However, you don't have to give up your routines; just change them up a bit. The idea here is to force your mind to be present and think about what you are doing. You may even discover a better way of doing the same thing. If you are always controlling your next step, you will only go as far as you know, but being open to new possibilities can allow you to go further than you imagined.

Try using a different route to work or home. Choose to dine at a different restaurant and try a new cuisine. Go to a networking event where you don't know anyone and leave with at least three new contacts. Change your desktop wallpaper. Sit at a different desk in your office, or better yet, sit outside if the weather or environment allows it. Change the furniture around in your house or apartment. Try a new exercise routine. Instead of a movie, read a book that relates to the movie. Instead of YouTube, try listening to a podcast and vice versa.

Taking your brain off of autopilot allows for provocative thinking. It causes your creativity to be engaged even if it's at a minimal level. I tried to introduce a sort of "earth hour" program in our home on Wednesday evenings from 7:00 p.m. It went well the first few times and we came up with interesting and unique ways to engage with each other. It only lasted for a while but we're now trying a variation of it.

Takeaways

A creative lifestyle requires courage and boldness as there is no evidence or guarantee of a set outcome. Be keen to observe the patterns in your life and extrapolate the lessons learned in line with your mission, and allow your creativity to be expressed not just in obvious creative activities but in many areas of your life

Your message to others and your contributions to life should not be taken lightly. Exploring the sparks from your creative gene will enhance your life and elevate you on many fronts.

The world is never oversaturated with creative ideas; there is a special place just for you. And once you blow the lid off and begin experimenting and expressing your creative genius, the more successful you will be. And you will find yourself collaborating more with others and finding solutions to problems.

Research on insightful problem solving, creative cognition, and acquisition of expertise, as well as historic case studies of individuals with exceptional creative accomplishments have replaced the view that the creative act is a mysterious or even mystical event.[27]

Embrace both the acquisition of knowledge and continuous trial and error.

Referring back to the Creative Careers study, Weinberg stated, "Our research suggests that when you're most creative is less a product of the scientific field that you're in, and is more about how you approach the work you do."

---

[27] Simonton, D. K. (2000). "Creativity: Cognitive, personal, developmental, and social aspects." American Psychologist, 55, 151–158. doi:10.1037/0003-066X.55.1.151.

NOTES

CHAPTER 7

Doing It!

Understanding the Steps and Misteps of Living Creatively!

*"Knowing is not enough; we must apply. Willing is not enough; we must do." — **Johann Wolfgang von Goethe***

Loggers in North America would use the various river networks to transport the logs quickly and efficiently. Picture all those logs flowing with the current down the river. But occasionally, a log jam would occur, paralyzing any further movement. An inexperienced logger would take a long time to figure out why the logs weren't moving, but an experienced logger would climb a very high tree to pinpoint the cause of the log jam. What they were looking for was the "key log" that was causing the jam. Once this key log was straightened out, the river would continue its work of transporting the logs.

In our lives, we all have logs that cause logjams and slow down our creative progress. In this chapter, as much as we will look at actions that can be performed to improve the quality of our lives, we must look at the actions in the context of right thinking, in the context of strategic thinking. Just like the experienced logger who climbs the high tree, we will go high to get a bird's-eye view of our situation and discover that key log. I will introduce several principles...

ɛɔ

The Vital Few

The Pareto Principle, commonly known as the 80/20 rule, is "the principle of the vital few." This principle teaches us that 80% of our results or effects stem from 20% of our effort; i.e., about 20% of the things we do are the critical few things that are responsible for the majority of our results. Continuing with our key log scenario, just sorting out the key log removes the log jam and allows all the other logs to flow smoothly. As you begin your creative journey, you will need to complement the blowing of the lid phase with a key log phase.

ɛɔ

Minor Adjustments => Major Improvements (MAMI)

1. It is from the 80/20 principle that I drew my inspiration for my signature principle or mantra, and I call it MAMI—which stands for "Minor Adjustments give Major Improvements." A major challenge that we face in our fast-paced life is that our activities lead us to always be busy but not necessarily productive.

   Don't get me wrong; as a transformational and turnaround specialist, I advocate for quantum leaps. To be successful and to be a high achiever requires more than just activity and being busy; it requires focus, discipline, and mastery. Mastery happens through a series of minor adjustments. If you want your creativity to blossom, you need to stop majoring in minor things.

Minor Adjustments => Major Improvements in Creativity

1. Instead of trying to master your time and schedule, learn to master your energy.

Stop trying to fill your daily calendar with so many creative things. You may have a master schedule but if you don't take into consideration your energy, moods, and circumstances, you won't be as creative or as productive as you could be. Learn how to distinguish activity from productivity. Ask yourself the simple question: Will this result in activity or productivity? Consider what I call your energy map—knowing when and where you are most energized. In the morning, evening, after a good sleep, after a good workout? Schedule time to reenergize yourself. Don't wait until you're tired; instead, schedule it into your day. For example, schedule a 10-minute break where you go for a walk, or stretch, or just relax your mind before moving on to the next "activity."

Take time to consider the finer details with an inquisitive mind. Think about what you need to achieve in the next hour. Perhaps, what you are doing now is not really tiring; perhaps, it just doesn't excite or energize you but instead sucks the energy out of you. Routine, mundane tasks are good examples of energy-sucking activities. You have to balance your schedule with energizing activities—activities that are part of your creative journey.

While you may be drawn to expend most of your energy on activities that have proven to spur your creativity, also take the time to go outside your comfort zone in order to further enhance your creative spark. Move from the tentative room, the room of experimentation, to the room of transformation. Through a series of iterations, you will discover that the person you need to be in order to take you where you want to go is not the person you are now.

Don't work hard; don't even work smart; just be hard working and pursue excellence. Be committed to your journey and look for ways to continually improve and challenge yourself.

2. *"Do the difficult things while they are easy, and do the great things while they are small. A journey of a thousand miles must begin with a single step"* – **Lao Tzu**

Don't let things pile up. Do you have small, simple things that you keep putting off because they are just easy and you know you can do them any time? Well, this could be contributing to you feeling overwhelmed and trapped in a cycle of activity. Find a way to get them done. As for difficult tasks, don't try to achieve a task all in one go; break it up into smaller, easier steps. Also, most difficult things get harder the longer you wait to get them done. Or perhaps you don't get things done when they are easy because you have not learned to schedule your time in collaboration with your energy; therefore, you become exhausted and put things off for another time. Without concrete deadlines, it's just human nature to keep putting things off. "Someday" is a day only found in the calendar of the unsuccessful.

3. Make progress, not perfection. Start where you are.

Everything is intertwined, and the reason you put off things more and more may be that you are trying to perfect them instead of simply making progress. This puts you in a vulnerable position. Being creative is often an area of uncharted waters; learn to embrace the idea of making attempts and failing. You don't fail when you have not yet accomplished something; you fail when you quit. When you take one step at a time and value progress over perfection, you strengthen your motivation and personal resolve to keep going. Progress is one of the greatest motivational tools. Picasso didn't create his best masterpiece on his first attempt. As my mentor James Karundu says, "Clarity comes when you start the journey."

Have you ever noticed that we often times come face-to-face with the exact obstacle we need at just the right time to sharpen us where we need it most? That is when you should MAMI it (Minor Adjustments => Major Improvements) and not be afraid of failure. Challenges and setbacks are intended to teach us something. They prepare us to perform more effectively at the next level. As someone once said, "Obstacles are the raw materials of great accomplishments."

4. Get help—stop flying solo.

You don't know everything, and even if you did, you can't go through the journey alone. The difficult tasks get even more difficult when you fly solo. Get the help you require from those who are aligned with, and in tune with, your objectives. Help will make your tasks more enjoyable and also hold you accountable and keep you focused. Of course, I realize that sometimes it can be difficult to find appropriate support for your creative aspirations. This is why I am starting this movement—to form a community of like-minded people on a similar journey who provide each other with social and practical support. Join the movement today! https://mailchi.mp/ce4a0dc12e5d/blowthelidoff.

5. Stop seeking validation from the wrong (negative) people.

One reason you might be stuck creatively is that you keep seeking validation from people who don't understand or share your particular creative genius. This is why some may refer to your ideas as crazy. It's crazy for them because they are stuck thinking in the metaphorical box and their creative gene is being suppressed or they want you to stay within their comfort zone. Surround yourself with people who appreciate your creative genius and who will not say, "It can't be done." Instead they will say, "How can I help you to get it done?" or perhaps "This is what I did, and it seemed to work."

6. Nurture your roots.

Recall our flowerpot and roots conversation in Chapter 4 where we were blowing the lid off. Because we have removed the limits of the flowerpot, you need to ensure that you work on getting your roots firmly grounded. I know you are filled with excitement about your newly discovered creativity. However, your new ideas are just seeds at this stage, and seeds are meant to be planted, fed, and nurtured so as to establish strong roots.

Some of you may have already started the journey and this book is helping you to cement your position. But no matter what stage you find yourself in, don't fall into the trap of measuring growth merely through what appears above the surface and failing to see that the real growth happens downwards—into the ground. The quantity and quality of produce that will grow later on is determined and encoded at this early stage of growth. This is why when you think nothing is happening with a tree, you are shocked when it magically begins to produce fruit in abundance.

Nurture the root and you'll always have fruit. Ignore the root—and say goodbye to the fruit!

❧

Clutter

One of the enemies of creative thinking is clutter. Nature doesn't like a vacuum, so if you don't utilize your space well, something will creep in and occupy that space. This often occurs when there is a lack of focus.

Usually, when we talk about clutter, we think of an untidy room. Although some may argue that a cluttered room is a great example of a creative space, I beg to differ. Untidiness signals confusion and chaos. The manner in which you keep physical things is typically a reflection of how you manage intangible things in your life. When you are used to just pushing things aside and not thinking about how they should be kept or leaving them for "later," you train your brain to respond in like manner to other things. And then your comfort zone and default settings become programmed.

*"Clutter is not just physical stuff. It's old ideas, toxic relationships and bad habits. Clutter is anything that does not support your better self." – **Eleanor Brown***

Here are some quick things you can do to declutter your life.

1. *Clothes.* Go through your closets and drawers (including shoes) and set aside clothes you don't actually use, whether or not you really like them. Put them nicely together and donate them to an institution or person who really needs them.

    Try not to go shopping for new clothes to replace the ones you have given away. Take time to enjoy your closet not being full. This is a subtle hint to you that in your lifestyle you now have more space. Intentionally fill it with things that support your creativity.

2. *Emails.* If you are someone who has the scary 6,000 unread emails, this is for you. How did you even get so many unread emails? Is it that you have subscribed to so many alerts but don't even read them? Whatever your reasons might be, this state represents many instances of inaction. You need to weed out the habit of inaction through this exercise. Be-

fore you jump the gun, I am not going to ask you to set time aside and read all those unread emails. What I will ask you to do is to simply go into your inbox and filter unread emails that are older than two months, select ALL, and then mark them as read! That's it. Done!

I know you might be wondering, "But what if I miss an important email in that mix?" Well, if you haven't read it in the last two months, what are the chances of you reading it anytime soon?

There are many other areas in your life that will need to be decluttered, so write them down and work on them. Take time to analyze where you need to create room, and then make a plan to get it done. Don't overthink it; just be brave enough to create your uncluttered lifestyle.

℘

Leadership

To make your great ideas truly become reality, it will require you to get rid of the clutter so you have the time and the energy to do what you really want to be doing. Blowing the lid off must involve the clearing of clutter that will hinder you from focusing on materializing your great ideas and letting your light shine.

Creativity requires transformational leadership. It requires you to summon courage from within and live the life you want to live! As my mentor James Karundu says, "Do your thing, do it your way and do it now!"

And remember that you are the leader of you!

So as not to confuse leadership with management, here is a short table distinguishing the two.

Leader	Manager
1. People follow them—vision creator	1. People work for them—goals creator
2. Change agent	2. Maintains status quo
3. No title required	3. Title is required and important
4. About what you do	4. About what you can get done through others
5. No experience required	5. Experience typically required for consideration
6. Influences people	6. Management of people and resources
7. Based on trust	7. Based on control
8. Develops principles and guidelines	8. Develops policies and procedures
9. Risk taker	9. Controls risk
10. Coaches	10. Directs

☙

Know Your Story

In 2001, I was employed as a computer sales executive on the island of Antigua. Let me give you some quick facts as to where the world was technologically in 2001.

- There were no iPhones.
- Bill Gates unveiled the first ever Xbox.
- Bluetooth wireless technology was just starting to be used.
- Microsoft XP was released.

- Everyone was on Napster.
- When you opened your word processor, Clippy (the paper clip helper) would ask you questions.
- Compaq Presario was released for the first time.
- The first iPod hit the market.
- Dell was the largest PC company.
- Most people were still on dial-up with a 56K modem.
- Nokia 3310, just released the year before, was the top selling mobile phone.

Although PC sales in the US had started declining, it was only now picking up in other places, such as in the twin island Caribbean state of Antigua and Barbuda. Having learned how to use the typewriter in high school, as well as having had a basic intro to computers, I was convinced that the future had arrived. In the early '90s, something impressed on my father that computers were the way to go and he enrolled my brother and I in an MS-DOS class. The resource book was as thick as an encyclopedia. Using floppy disks was a mark of superior computing skills.

So when I got the computer sales job in 2001, it was an exciting job. I had no formal training in sales and marketing but I had a passion for technology and enjoyed speaking to people (well, more of a chatterbox actually). I noticed most of the interested individuals were high school students but they didn't have the purchasing power. Somehow, even back then, I understood how to filter the enquiries of individuals with a genuine desire to purchase compared to those who were just intrigued. Once I identified this niche, I made a plan for how to approach them en masse by going to their schools. I approached several affluent high schools and sold the idea to the principals that I could speak to the student body about how this new technology was the future and would greatly help them in their research and other school assignments.

Before each speech to the students, I would be creative regarding how to capture their attention by giving a motivational introduction. And at the end, I would give them three quick pointers to help them convince their parents to make the purchase and then send them home with supporting flyers and documentation. This plan worked well and I was able not only to make a number of sales but also to have an impact on many with my speeches. I also landed several radio spots talking about computers. This was actually the point in my life where my speaking career began, as I was able to do it with ease and flair and in my own unique way.

In 2007, I was employed as a public high school teacher responsible for rolling out the teaching of computer science to students in Form 1 (the first year of high school in Antigua). Included in this roll-out was the use of the first electronic white board in public schools. In order to get the students to have a more practical approach to learning how computers function, I would go with an old computer and strip it down to its component parts. In the higher classes, we went over and above the teaching syllabus and taught students how to assemble and disassemble the computer. The Ministry of Education would later decide, during its annual science and computer fair, to include a speed competition to assemble and disassemble computers. Our students placed first across all age groups.

Unleashing your creativity may require you to be a kind of "éminence grise" with your impact.

"Every closed door isn't locked and even if it is...YOU just might have the key! Search within to unlock a world of possibilities!" – ***Sanjo Jendayi***

Be brave enough to be you, to do things your way, to stand out from the crowd, to take on the challenges and barriers that others think cannot be overcome. Pick your lane and stick to it.

Understand that your journey is unique because you are unique; therefore, the opportunities and challenges that may appear standard to many will benefit you more when you allow your uniqueness to lead your march to victory. Be a leader without a title. Do things that have not been done before or that people don't really understand.

Creativity is using your unique combination of knowledge, experience, and imagination to light up the world with new possibilities. No one else has your combination, so don't rob the world of your creativity. No one else can get your idea out there in the way you envision it. Put it out there and run with it. At times, you have to be the entrepreneur of your creative ideas, even if you are an employee and the ideas are for the company's benefit.

These are critical (minor or major) adjustments you will need to make as you proceed with your journey. The desire to get to the next level will demand a new you. The person that got you to where you are now will not be the person you will be at your next level. Let the escape from poverty and fear get you started, but then let the pursuit and fulfilment of your purpose propel you and never let you quit.

Transform from hesitation to chasing your dreams. From surviving to thriving. From working to building and creating. From living to legacy.

❧

Goals

As your creativity begins to blossom, you then need to set beacons as the desired destinations for your creative ideas.

The ability to set and achieve goals is underpinned by planning. Mastering planning is the key to success in any aspect of life. It fosters the discipline and persistence required to winning and achieving.

We will not be focusing on the traditional tenets of goal setting, such as what is a goal, how to set and measure your goals, etc.; instead, I will draw your attention to the spirit of goal setting and why it is important.

More often than not, we focus our energies on setting and achieving the wrong type of goals—goals that are events or occasions as opposed to journey-type goals. For example, most people have more detailed goals for their wedding rather than their marriage, for their diets rather than their lifestyle, for holidays, and not for their everyday life. Again, majoring in minor things. Your goal setting should not be constrained to such a myopic perspective. Let your goal setting and planning support the crafting of your creativity.

How will goal setting actually help me?

When goal setting is done right, i.e., done in a SMART manner (specific, measurable, achievable, realistic, and timebound), it catalyzes your brain and activates your GPS. You then focus your energies on achieving those goals. More importantly, you will begin to take personal responsibility for your life and its outcomes. You are more aware of opportunities that will get you where you need to be and move you away from allowing life to toss you here, there, and everywhere.

"The number one reason people don't set goals is that they have not yet accepted personal responsibility for their lives."
– **Tommy Newberry**

Do I need to have my goals written down?

Absolutely. When you write your goals down—as you did in Chapter 5 and on social media with the hashtag #BlowThe-LidOff—you enter into an accountability contract with yourself to be responsible to achieve those goals. You can send me an email (Robert@RobertABelle.com) if you need an accountability partner. It's just like when you are brainstorming ideas and you jot down everything that comes to mind. Seeing those ideas on paper gives you a new perspective and solidifies your thoughts. This strengthens your discipline and your character. It activates your brain's RAS (reticular activating system)—the mechanism within your brain that controls your awareness. Seeing where you are and where you need to be creates a kind of tension in your brain. To relieve this tension, your brain will become more alert to people, resources, and opportunities that align with and will help you to achieve your goals.

We have so many things running through our minds in this fast-paced world—and this can easily lead to your goals being drowned by the stress and cares of life if they simply remain in your thoughts and are not captured—that is written down either manually or electronically.

Recall a time when you achieved a goal that you set out to achieve. How did you feel? While recently clearing out some old papers, I found a notebook in which I had written my goals five years ago. As it turned out, I had achieved every single one of those goals, some as recently as a few months ago. That felt great!

Remember that answers always follow reasons. Get the why and then you will figure out the how. Goals that take you out of your comfort zone activate your natural creativity, supplying you with insights for achieving your goals that otherwise would not have occurred to you. Be careful of letting limits turn into excuses that eventually spoil your opportunities for getting more out of life. Vague and hazy objectives produce diluted results! You'll find that your creativity will increase as you define your goals more clearly.

๛

Fear of Failure?

No one likes to fail and that is why we fear setting big goals, having big dreams, and living more creatively. Playing it safe usually seems like the safer option and indeed it is. It safely keeps you within your comfort zone and locks you out of achieving great things.

The creative journey can involve any number of setbacks or failures along the way. You will have to learn how to interact with setbacks and failures, so let's set some ground rules on how we will interact with failure.

Have you ever observed someone learning to ride a bicycle? For the learner, it is scary and wobbly the first few times as they try to keep their balance, but the strategy for them is not to stop but rather to keep pedaling, to keep moving. Even when a child takes the training wheels off and the adult is there holding the bike, the fear of falling is still present in the child's mind and he may be constantly looking down, anticipating the fall. This can only be overcome, however, if he keeps his eyes focused on where he is going and trusts his guide to help him maintain his balance.

Hey, no one has ever learned to ride a bike without falling, so the sooner you accept that you will fall, the sooner you can get back up and keep moving. Don't be tempted to acquire all the knowledge in the world about bike riding before you attempt your first ride. Gather sufficient information and just start, experience your falls, and get up and keep moving.

You could get a "master's degree" in bike riding—all the knowledge you could ever need—but until you sit on that seat, grip those handles, and place your feet on the pedals, you will not accomplish anything worthwhile.

Failure is the fuel of mastery. Learning to accept and handle failure, and to carry on with your initiative, will elevate you to unimaginable heights.

Similarly, this book is meant to be your launch pad into creative living. Don't for a moment think you need to read more books or acquire more knowledge—start now! Begin the transformation today!

Referring back to our Four C Model of Creativity, one vital ability that will help you to progress in the creative journey is creative self-efficacy. Creative self-efficacy refers to the confidence that people have in their ability to generate new and meaningful ideas.[32] [33] Creative self-efficacy requires the creator to have confidence, courage, and the willingness not only to engage in creative activities but also to discuss and explore creativity with others. And it requires being open to receiving feedback on one's insights and ideas.

At times, though, we confuse our failures with mistakes. A mistake is an action that can be corrected. Therefore, if we can take a step back and learn to identify our mistakes earlier, it will help us to avoid failures. Of course, this is so much easier said than done; it is human nature to explain away our mistakes instead of accepting them and learning from them but we can make a commitment to try.

It can be hard to admit when you make a mistake, and so my advice is to always have an accountability partner who can help you identify your mistakes, and then you can make the necessary corrections. Take a coach, for example; a coach will hold your hand and walk with you but will not let you off the hook easily. A

---

[32] R.A. Beghetto, "Creative self-efficacy: Correlates in middle and secondary students," Creativity Research Journal, 18 (4) (2006), pp. 447-457.

[33] P. Tierney, S.M. Farmer, "Creative self-efficacy: Its potential antecedents and relationship to creative performance," Academy of Management Journal, 45 (6) (2002), pp. 1137-1148.

coach helps you identify your mistakes and correct them, and then get ready for the next level of success.

Learning is generally believed to occur based on the 70/20/10 model, as described by Lombardo and Eichnger (1996). This model states that people effectively learn as follows:

- 70% from challenging assignments
- 20% from developmental relationships
- 10% from coursework and training

If we apply this model, doing challenging assignments will teach you so much more than acquiring more knowledge. In case you haven't done the "blow-the-lid-off" assignment in Chapter 5, go back and get it done. If you have completed it, don't let your lack of knowledge on whatever subject matter hold you back—get started today.

Remember to post your results using hashtag #BlowTheLidOff so we can celebrate you. Also, your learning should not end after reading this book; that's why I want you to sign up for my newsletter on https://mailchi.mp/ce4a0dc12e5d/blowthelidoff.

Here are some pitfalls to avoid as you journey to incorporate your creativity into your life. You may find yourself at some point in the future ready to take your creative genius into a profitable business idea. This is my hope for you as you read this book—to receive a reward or rewards for your brilliant or crazy ideas. Well, here are what I consider to be the common mistakes that creative type businesses make and how you can avoid them.

ᖇᐧᓄ

Costly Mistakes Creatives Make, and How to Avoid Them

Running a creative business can be compared to a car—with the technical/creative aspect of the business being the engine, the finances being the tires, the processes being the oil, the reports being like the dashboard, and finally, the Intellectual Property being like the motor vehicle insurance.

1) Overemphasizing building your talent (Engine)

While as a creative you need to work on and improve your talent, too often creatives and service providers do this to the detriment of building their business. Creativity, no matter how brilliant it is, does not exist in a vacuum. It needs a structure to support it, market it, and provide it to others to consume. This then leads to a heavy reliance on others for the success of your business. It doesn't mean that you need to be a jack of all trades but you do need to get involved and move outside of your comfort zone.

The mistake of not having a structure is like wanting the engine of the car to go faster and faster but without knowing where it is you want to get to and without proper supporting parts. This is perhaps the biggest and most costly mistake, as it has long-lasting ripple effects on the growth of your business.

2) Not having a financial structure (Tires) in place

Having the right tire (size and type), depending on the terrain and the distance, can greatly improve your car's performance. Also, understanding the pressure level required for the load of the car is a minor adjustment that can mean major improvement. Insufficient psi leads to an increase in fuel consumption. Similarly, a business that doesn't have the right mix of liquid-illiquid cash, or short-term and long-term investments that match the needs of the business, can become a barrier to your business growth as cash wastage will increase.

Many creatives are too busy being creative, perhaps to the point where they don't even keep a record of the income/expenses in their business. This leads to the notorious question of: "Where has all my money gone?" Imagine not being able to know who owes you and how much. This problem is not isolated to creative type businesses, however. Many businesses struggle with high debt or a case of bad debt.

This mistake is further exasperated when the creative doesn't clearly separate their personal expenditures and those of the business. This is why having an appropriate structure and support system for accountability is crucial. We see cases of talented musicians, athletes, and creatives going bankrupt or being in trouble for failure to pay the correct amount of taxes. Also, not keeping a record of when business money is used for personal expenditures is a common problem—the biggest financial threat to any business is, surprisingly, the owner! No one is there to question you on how and when you spend your money.

Back to our car scenario, if you don't check the pressure and condition (tread levels) of your tires regularly, your car will most likely be operating below the optimum level and worst case, you will find yourself stuck on the road with a flat tire. This is directly relevant to a business, as lack of financial structure can cause your business to come to a grinding halt!

3) Lack of a focused self-care process (Oil)

The oil in a car needs to be changed and refreshed based on the usage of the car and the work the engine has done. A creative must have a process where they can "break away" from the routine and take time for self-care! This is a critical process as it allows the mind and heart to be reenergized, which will lead to more creative thinking and content creation.

I am a big proponent of self-care as I see the benefits it provides to me in my creative process. Self-care must include an element of unplugging. I find that one of the best ways to unplug is by being out in nature or by being physically active. As much as I enjoy speaking, I can't speak every day of the year.

"Solitude is creativity's best friend, and solitude is refreshment for our souls." – **Naomi Judd**

I find that when I exercise, my mind becomes clearer and my stress levels are drastically reduced. The blood in our bodies is meant to keep moving and there is no better way to get the heart "pumping" than to exercise. Exercise also causes the release of serotonin and endorphins, which are known as the feel-good hormones. I find that ideas tend to flow better after a great workout session or time in nature. If you have not been incorporating exercise into your routine, I urge you to start.

I also want to challenge you to learn to be unavailable during those times when you are having an exercise break. What about emergencies, you may ask? Well, are what you call "emergencies" really emergencies or are they just a lack of proper planning by yourself (probably) or others? Being unavailable for a limited amount of time trains those who constantly run to you for solutions to realize that you need time to recharge and be refreshed and that they need to work around your schedule as much as possible.

While writing this book and attending to other life demands, I began to feel overwhelmed. Warning lights on my life dashboard! So I knew I needed to unplug and get away from the frenzy of urbanization and constant connectivity. I told my family that I was going on a solo trip and I booked a flight to the southern coast of Kenya.

For three days, I switched my phone off (after letting my family and friends know in which hotel I was staying, in case of emergencies). For the entire trip, I did absolutely nothing. Despite my room being beachside, I didn't even set foot in the ocean. No movies, no books, nothing. Just walking, going to the spa, connecting to nature, listening to the waves crashing and the birds singing. They do say time flies when you are having a good time, and indeed it did. I was shocked at how quickly the time went.

You need to find and develop an "oil changing" process that works for you.

4) Not having someone (like a professional) to hold your hand, help you deal with your problems, and keep you accountable (a mechanic)

You need a mentor who will assist you with your business and help you to stretch your comfort zone by improving your confidence in vulnerable areas, such as finance, marketing, and taxes. Find a business mentor with whom you can do regular check-ins but also one whom you can run to in the event of a problem or "accident."

5) Insufficient self-belief

This is perhaps the single biggest killer in any creative business!

I find that what underlies this problem is the mismatch between what the creative knows (skills, talents, abilities) and what is actually produced (output). As a creative, you have so many life-changing ideas and talents that you want to get going with and you may want to do it all at once. (The vicious cycle of Mistake #1). This leads to procrastination as you worry that your idea is not actually ready when compared with the more experienced players in the industry and the desire to produce output at that level at the very first or first few attempts becomes the goal! Evidence of this is seen in statements such as "I am an upcoming artist" or "I am an aspiring photographer." You rob the world of experiencing your creative idea as you try to perfect it. Don't be selfish with your creativity—share it with us.

While I am all for benchmarking and striving for excellence, as a creative you need to first start with the many rough edges and then MAMI.

Being ready is a decision you make and not a position to arrive at!

Be cautioned, however, to ensure that you develop the knowledge to understand when to and when not to release your creative offering. Having this knowledge describes someone with creative metacognition (CMC). Employing strategies for how to be creative in your specific context, coupled with skills such as self-awareness and self-reflection, and balancing the risk and rewards in order to reap the most benefits will allow your creative ideas to flourish. Your creative ideas can be disruptive, and while this may be beneficial at times, it can also result in dangerous responses. Perhaps, the possibility of this fear is one of the reasons that holds us back from expressing our creative ideas. I refer to this as "knowing how to tell your story." As I mentor other accountants and finance professionals, one of my key objectives is to teach them how best to tell their stories, not just the story of the numbers, but the meaning behind those numbers and how their insights can help create a "happy ending."

Get started today and produce that art *now.*

Share with us your output using the hashtag #BlowTheLidOff, and feel free to send me an email at Robert@robertabelle.com so I can celebrate you and give you a shout-out.

The most novice product produced is always better than the greatest idea stuck in someone's mind. That's why we have prototyping—to help get user feedback and fuel iterations. In other words, MAMI (Make minor adjustments that will give you major improvements).

So you are back in that perfect point in a meeting or conversation, and you boldly answer the creative call. You no longer wish to ignore the ringing sounds in your head. Of course, you need a strategy to be able to get past that scary point. In a corporate setting, you can rehearse how you will voice your ideas. Or perhaps you are more introverted and would want to first synthesize the idea, then craft a strategy that allows you to at least mention the idea, and then request time to fine-tune it further in a follow-up email. Also, finding a partner who is more comfortable doing presentations might be a good strategy. However, there will be times when you will need to do it on your own. This will likely be a scary moment, but if you are not doing scary things, then you are not growing. Doing scary things forces you to be intentional about your growth and development and it can help you unleash your creative force. Allow your need to solve the problem to be greater than your fear of externalizing it.

Enter Your Flow State

You may have experienced a time when you were so engulfed in your activity that your thoughts, words, and actions just keep flowing seamlessly. So much so that you might even have forgotten to do things such as eating. It's like when someone says they are in the zone.

Psychologist Mihály Csíkszentmihályi was the first to identify and research this phenomenon of flow state. His interest in art led him to wonder how painters such as Michelangelo did what they did. He also interviewed musicians, athletes, and artists. Having identified his purpose, the problem of low levels of happiness in Hungary propelled him. He wanted to discover what piques creativity and how it can be replicated. Mihály concluded that the key to happiness is to enter into a flow state, therefore, controlling the contents of your consciousness instead of being passively controlled by external forces.

Circling back to Maslow's hierarchy of needs, a self-actualized person is one who is creative. Being creative allows you to develop the contents of your consciousness by entering into a flow state and this leads to happiness that is not an external state of being but rather an internal one.

"The best moments in our lives are not the passive, receptive, relaxing times…The best moments usually occur if a person's body or mind is stretched to its limits in a voluntary effort to accomplish something difficult and worthwhile."[34]

These are the eight characteristics of flow according to Csíkszentmihályi:

1. Complete concentration on the task

2. Clarity of goals, reward in mind, and immediate feedback

3. Transformation of time (speeding up/slowing down)

4. The experience is intrinsically rewarding

5. Effortlessness and ease

6. There is a balance between challenge and skills

7. Actions and awareness are merged, losing self-conscious rumination

8. There is a feeling of control over the task

---

[34] Csikszentmihalyi, Mihaly (1990). Flow: The Psychology of Optimal Experience. New York, NY: Harper and Row.

Takeaways

In a creative life, it is critical to understand the importance of both action and inaction to spurring creativity. Setting goals aligned to your mission allows your creativity to kick in and get you to your desired result. At this point, you need to get lost in action or you will perish in despair. Use and master the MAMI principle to keep you moving, like riding a bicycle.

Setting goals and planning are the two key skills that will help you create the roadmap to bring your creative ideas to life; they will allow you to materialize your creativity.

Failure is a part of the deal, but failure is not defeat. It is an opportunity to make corrections and then keep going. Progress must always supersede perfection as you execute your tasks and actions, knowing that anything worth doing is worth doing poorly at first. Perfection is a later stage.

NOTES

CHAPTER 8

Monetizing It!
The Crafting and Reward Cycle!

"A compelling offer is 10 times better than a convincing argument." – **Dean Jackson**

In the 1970s, an advertiser named Gary Ross Dahl devised a new type of pet, the perfect pet, a pet never before seen or imagined—a Pet Rock! It was an idea that started over drinks with friends as they complained about their pets. Then Dahl reconsidered his goofy idea of a pet rock and decided to take himself seriously. He worked on sourcing the stones and he came up with a unique idea for packaging and presentation.

Dahl sold the Pet Rock for $3.95, averaging about $3.00 profit on each unit. Within about six months of the Pet Rocks being available in stores, Dahl had made approximately $5 million. It was a fad that only lasted for about a year and then it died off.

The Pet Rock also came with a comical instruction manual of commands like "sit here," "come," "roll over," and "play," and the manual was full of puns and jokes. Dahl boasted that this was the perfect pet that didn't need to be fed, walked, bathed, or taken to the vet.

"I packaged a sense of humor for a very bored public," Dahl admitted in an interview with the *Oakland Tribune*. Americans had just come out of the Vietnamese War, the Watergate Scandal, and a recession. People needed humor and laughter and that's what Dahl gave them. The success of the Pet Rock was due to the power of marketing and positioning, and there are actually marketing books that teach the Pet Rock marketing strategy. Considered to be one of the worst products ever, the Pet Rock fad demonstrated that a questionable product or idea can be successful with great marketing.

Conversely, there are many stories of seemingly great and innovative products failing due to poor positioning, marketing, or timing.

∽

It's Worth Something!

So here you are living your life and using some of those crazy ideas you wrote down during the blow-the-lid-off exercise, and it's exciting—maybe even exhilarating sometimes—but will someone pay for it? If you are new on this journey, you may not even be aware of how powerful and valuable your ideas are. Maybe you don't even want to bring up the money conversation; you just want to share your art. You feel vulnerable asking for compensation for your work or services. And the annoying imposter syndrome fly buzzes in your ear, "Why should anyone pay you for this? What qualifications do you have? Are you popular enough or known enough to market your product...or to charge that much?"

You may not comprehend the value you are providing by letting your light shine. You are creating original ideas, solving problems for people, and you even get comments like, "You should be charging people for this," or "If you would sell these solutions, I would pay a premium for them."

You ponder these questions as you hear the testaments that you are adding value to someone's life, but you are not sure how to go about monetizing your creativity. You feel so uncomfortable charging for your work. This could be as a result of you thinking that money isn't everything, and indeed it isn't, but money received is feedback for value provided. However, this won't happen until you travel through the vulnerable valley and ascend to the victory mountain. Well, I am here to tell you that indeed your creativity is worth something! You should be getting paid for your ideas; you need to activate the money flow.

One of the assignments I give my creative clients relates to pricing strategies. This involves them either starting to charge for their work or raising their prices. At times, I don't apply a formula and just use the "gut feeling" approach so I can get them moving out of the vulnerable valley. I also ask them to ask their clients who are willing to be open with them about how much they would be willing to pay. I have found this to be the scariest part of their creative journey. When there is a negative relationship with money and pricing and with general financial management, not only does the starving artist syndrome occur but also the artists who are in business may close their doors, reduce their output, or completely stop.

Don't get stuck in the *vulnerable valley* hiding behind rocks. Read on and move to the *victory mountain.*

༄

Sales and Marketing

When any product is bought or sold, it is as a result of both marketing and selling. This does not mean that you need a certificate or a degree in sales and marketing, but you *do* need to understand how customers and consumers will interact with you in order for you to be able to sell them your creative idea.

This also does not mean that you need to be a great public speaker or a great salesperson. Outside of business, we are always marketing or selling something. If you are employed or have ever been employed, then you did some sales and marketing to get that job. If you are in a relationship or married, there was some form of marketing that took place, although it was obviously packaged differently. And the friends that you have are also a result of you marketing yourself, displaying who you are—although you probably didn't think of it that way.

To get a better understanding of my customers, I use a principle I call "the substitutive principle." In this principle, I flip the script and put myself in the shoes of the customer. I look at examples and draw lessons from when I was a customer. For instance, to understand sales and marketing better, I go back and think about a product that I bought and what were the various interactions I had with that product prior to purchasing it.

Selling includes the activities you perform when you are in contact with your prospective customer and intent on convincing them to make the purchase. At this stage, you are answering last minute doubts around the purchasing decision. Selling is not forcing a customer to make a purchase; the premise here is that they are in the process of making a final decision but might need a little more convincing, assurance, or information before making up their mind.

Marketing is the activities you do that are designed to target the right customer, get the customer in contact with you, and ensure that your product is well positioned. When you position a product, you are ensuring that your brand takes a distinct position in the mind of the customer in relation to their needs and in relation to the competition.

So sales and marketing go hand in hand. But from now on, let's call it *"marketing and sales"* as you must first *market* your product before you work on making a *sale*.

❧

Obey the Line

One of the mistakes that is often made in marketing a creative idea, brand, or business is not observing and understanding the *line—the marketing line*. The marketing line divides marketing activities into two parts, based on two different objectives.

The two categories are:

Above-the-Line Marketing (ATL) – In ATL, activities are widespread and untargeted, thus trying to reach both customers and noncustomers and it is heavily focused on brand building. Companies who have dominant positions in the market usually focus more here so as to position and cement their brand in the market. Activities thus include outdoor advertising through big billboards, spreads in newspapers and other publications, and TV and radio commercials.

Below-the-Line Marketing (BTL) – Activities here target a specific group of people—a niche. This is direct marketing focused on conversions and repeat business. This means the messaging is specific and detailed, pointing out the problem issue and the solution being provided. It's also used as a rallying call for members of the *tribe* so they can benefit from the solution they have been waiting for with you.

Then there is the not-so-new segment of line marketing called *Through-the-Line,* which integrates activities of both ATL and BTL.

When we don't *obey the line* and end up playing more *above the line*, then we end up attracting more suspects than prospects. A *suspect* is a curious person and one who usually requires a whole lot of convincing to make a purchase. Whereas a *prospect* is highly interested but needs a little more reassurance regarding their fears or their unique requirements.

Let's Substitute. Think of when you see a billboard or a TV ad—how many times have you actually purchased the advertised item? Then think of when you have received a targeted advertisement and have found something that you probably didn't know existed but is just right for you. Social media has become one of the biggest marketplaces, coupled with the analytics of big data that hit us daily with BTL advertising. Check out a hotel or tourist spot in another country because one of your friends visited there and you'll start seeing flight and holiday packages popping up on your news feeds or banners. You may actually be thinking of travelling and you might get some great offers or you may not be interested at this time.

℘

Niche Marketing

Coming up with a creative, crazy idea can at times be difficult and at other times easy. But either way, revealing it is very exciting. The challenge can come when you reveal it to others (put it on the market) and it doesn't get much of a response. You then end up having to do a lot of explaining and convincing, and though this might result in a sale or two, it still does not return the results you were expecting. Yes, your idea is revolutionary, you have put a lot of work and time into it, and you know so many people who have this problem. You want to tell your friends, family, and anyone you come in contact with about this great idea.

We live in an age where the marketplace is very "noisy," and most people think that the best way to be noticed is to shout the loudest by doing big billboards and ATL marketing activities.

With this, however, you will be shouting louder at everyone and no one. If you have experienced such situations, I know the feelings of self-doubt and inadequacy that can begin to settle and take up residence in your mind.

After a while, you begin to excuse this seemingly poor performance by shifting the blame onto the market and the customers and saying things like, "They aren't ready for my idea yet," "People don't appreciate creativity and fine art," or "Customers don't realize how much this solution will help them."

Let's change that mindset NOW!

It's *your* job to help get the customers ready for your new idea, it's *your* responsibility to help them appreciate the value of your solution, and it's *your* task to help them understand the problem you are solving. And you do this through *your marketing communication.*

So now that we have accepted responsibility, let's see what we can do to change this narrative. As you have observed when reading this book, everything we do must be systematic and done with intention. Your creativity must be aligned with your *mission.* Therefore, monetizing that creativity must also be done with intent, i.e., it must be crafted. Crafting is a skill and a skill can be learned. Allow me to teach you how to do it.

Knowing how to communicate your messaging is not just about *how* you do it; it is also about *what* you are saying and *to whom* it is being said. Your prospective customers are not all at the same level of awareness. For instance, some of you reading my book may not believe that you are creative, and so your experience reading this book will definitely be different from the experience of the person who *knows* they are creative but they still need a push when it comes to marketing.

So let's look at some tactics you need to consider when crafting your marketing message.

☙

Who Is Your Niche?

A niche is a subset of a market with specific demographics. When you were thinking about your mission, what type of person came to your mind? What are their demographics, and what is the specific problem they are facing that fuels your creativity? Take a piece a paper and just start to write down what comes to your mind—write words, phrases, and anything else that pops up, but don't try to draft complete sentences at this time. One of the best tools I use for this is basically *market research*. And no, it's not limited to conducting surveys and questionnaires but simply by *listening*.

I used months of my time going out and attending conferences where I thought my niche market would be. I would just briefly mention something to do with my product and then let them talk. And I would listen, taking note of their intonations and the words that stirred them up when they said them.

I would then go home and compare the words and phrases I had used with the ones they had used, and over time I came up with my messaging. The risk here is that trying to be too creative or unique with your messaging can lead you to being out of touch with the language of your niche. You need to be able to *speak their language but in your style*. Also, always remember to KISS (keep it short and sweet).

Who is the niche for your great idea? As you discover the answer, go back and write next to each great idea specifically who your niche is. Spoiler alert: You won't get it right on the first try—or at least it won't be as detailed as it needs to be—well, unless you are absolutely sure. If you are, then I challenge you to reexamine it in light of this chapter.

Failure to take the time to understand your niche market will result in your message focusing more and more on "features" rather than on *benefits*. As I always say: in communication, the message is always about the *receiver*, so use language and whatever else will make it easier for the recipient to decode and understand it.

"People don't care how much you know until they know how much you care." – **Theodore Roosevelt**

Remember my computer sales experience in 2001? Others were busy talking about specs that the market didn't even understand at that time. Who understood what processor speeds and storage capacity really meant? Today if you tell me my computer has an HDD hard disk with 1 TB of storage, I can translate it and compare it to my needs, but back in those early days, people were not familiar with those concepts. They didn't know how much memory they needed or how the difference in storage would affect them. I would listen to the conversations, and when the sales exec would talk about storage, most of the responses would be, "Do you think that is enough?" The conversation would be long with lots of questions back and forth.

I chose to target high school students and particularly those in the upper classes. I first addressed their immediate need of doing more, faster and easier, and then I painted the picture of life after high school and what a desktop computer could do for them. I created a back-to-school package, and I spent very little time explaining or highlighting features and specs—only using them as a reference point regarding how they contributed to the overall solution and to differentiate the various products.

⁂

Habit #5: Seek First to Understand, Then to Be Understood

Stephen Covey, in his book, *The 7 Habits of Highly Effective People*, said:

"When we're communicating with another, we need to give full attention, to be

completely present. Then we need to empathize – to see from the other's point of

view, to 'walk in his moccasins' for a while. Until people feel that you

understand them, they will not be open to your influence."

The key to your influence with me is your understanding of *me*. Unless you understand me and my unique situation and feelings, you won't know how to advise or counsel me. Unless you're influenced by my uniqueness, I'm not going to be influenced by your advice. My attention hinges on my interests. So if you want my attention, appeal to my interests; then I will know you are worth my giving you some time."

You want to make a *connection* with your niche and not simply sell them something. You want them to *belong* to your journey or mission...

"I want to connect with you and to share more of my experiences with you."

"I want you to be a part of this movement, so keep posting using hashtag #BlowTheLidOff and let's encourage each other."

You might discover, in your attempts to find your niche, that *it doesn't actually exist*. That's okay; it just means that you have to *create* your niche. Sometimes, the people in a particular niche may not be aware of their problem and you can be the one to raise their awareness. Because we get accustomed to accepting things the way they are, we at times don't even consider an inconvenience to be a problem and we tell ourselves, "That's just the way it is." Before the internet, who would have thought that we needed it? And at first, there was resistance and a slow uptake of internet use. My mentor James Karundu says, "Where there is a calling, there is a craving." So don't worry if you can't find your niche; step out with your idea and see your niche develop right before your eyes.

ᕲᕳ

Value-Based Pricing

Once you have identified your niche and its characteristics, we can then more accurately determine an appropriate price point. Here are some things *not* to consider when pricing your creative product.

What the competition is charging. When you identify your niche and can clearly articulate the problem solution, it doesn't really matter what the competition is charging. They may not be solving the same problem or doing it the way you do it. Especially when your niche is not fully defined, you really can't price based on the competition. You can, however, use it to gauge your pricing level because you will need to be able to explain your reason for the variation from the market rate. If your price is higher, then your premium must be known, understood, and accepted by your niche market. If your price is lower, then your discount must be known, understood, and accepted by your niche market. Don't let the competition dictate your pricing. Competition helps to raise the market's awareness of the problem solution; all you have to do is to direct them to *you* and pricing can be one of those differentiating factors.

Negotiating. You give away your creativity for peanuts when you engage in a bargaining war with a customer. This is expressed through undercharging in an attempt to gain "more" customers instead of looking for the customers who will appreciate the value being created and compensate accordingly. We stated that *value* is created by solving a specific problem in your unique way—that's what the customer receives. Well, *price* is what the customer rewards you with for that value creation. If a customer insists on paying lower prices, it's because they don't recognize the value that has been created. Whether or not you have created the value is not the issue; if the customer does not recognize it, they won't be willing to reward you. Let's substitute...Have you ever felt that the price you paid for something didn't reflect the value you received from it and that the price could be higher? How about a recent purchase you made and you were convinced that the asking price was too high and you negotiated to bring the price down?

Time and effort taken. Another big mistake you can make in pricing is based on the time or energy put into the solution. As an accountant, I have no pricing based on the amount of time I will spend with a client unless this is stipulated based on law, legislation, or affiliate rules. Outside of that, I charge for my services based on value creation—by offering packages that clearly show the desired outcome. The *time formula* does not reward innovation because the less time you take, the less the reward. It doesn't take into account your creativity that allows you to get things done faster through automation or other means. Creativity, after all, is just connecting things. Steve Jobs said, "When you ask creative people how they did something, they may feel a little guilty because they didn't really do it; they just *saw* something. It seemed obvious to them after a while. That's because they were able to connect experiences they've had and synthesize new things."

Modesty. Being modest in pricing is actually detrimental because it clouds your judgment. It leads to ambiguity about money, which will tend to produce mixed results. If you believe that your creative idea is something that should be made freely available to all because it can save lives, then there are ways you can still monetize it, such as through social enterprise. However, from a commercial standpoint, this can reflect a lack of confidence in yourself and an inability to recognize your gifts and talents. In a creative world, satisfaction and acceptability of one's ideas is the best reward, but this reward is expressed more strongly through monetary terms. Don't get me wrong; I am not advocating that we should be extreme capitalists here. I am simply stating that you should be clear as to your money position. Of course, there are times I take assignments that don't offer monetary compensation, but I ensure that I am not allowing someone or an organization to take my creativity for granted.

Being stingy. Oftentimes, we want to receive top dollar for our creativity but we always want to pay a discount for others' creativity. I want to challenge you to be more mindful of your attitude as a customer. When you begin to appreciate and reward others for their creativity, you establish an aura of recognition for value creation. Have you ever noticed that you can tell when someone is selling something expensive but there is just something about them that makes you doubt they are being genuine? You find nothing visibly wrong with the product being offered but the person selling it just doesn't seem to connect with you.Creativity is not something that is offered off the shelf; it's something that requires a connection. It requires a deep and special connection, and there is no competition for special connections.

This is why I share my experiences with you in this book. I want you to be able to connect with me to see that we are not so different and that I understand where you are in your creative journey—as I have been there before. So don't be stingy with your experiences, and don't be stingy with your money when it comes to rewarding creativity.

Monetizing your creativity is a trial-and-error, hit-and-miss journey. It will take time to get it just right, and even then there will always be room for improvement. Here is one thing you can implement right away if you still aren't sure where to start. Just sit and think about your niche, your messaging, and the problem you are solving. Then trust your gut and pick a figure "out of the air." Use it as your new price and see how it goes. The fact is: While you think about your creativity and the impact it can have, your brain subconsciously begins to assign a monetary value—based on your life and monetary experience—to what you have to offer. We just have to tune in to our inner self. Of course, this is something scary to do, but I would urge you to try it and see what lessons you learn from the experience.

᨞

Bull's-Eye Focus – The Sweet Spot

You will have to keep trying and failing at this in order to get it right. You will also notice that your pricing journey goes hand in hand with your *"niche clarity journey."* The clearer you can get about your *niche,* the clearer you will be about your pricing. Consider a dartboard with its bull's-eye target. You can hit a zone close to the center and earn yourself a high score or a low score. But when you hit that small but sweet spot in the center of the board, you get the best reward—the highest score. However, it takes practice and a clear strategy to be able to hit that target. Similarly, you need focus, practice, and staying power to develop experience with your *niche* before you can establish credibility and become a recognized expert in solving their problems.

At this stage, you shift from merely solving their problems to providing a complete solution, as you get insights revealing that there are more possible issues and more room for improvement and creativity. Don't just meet their need; plant a seed—a seed of transformation where you can take them on a creative journey.

Once you find your "sweet spot," you will have improved customer relations, which is a component of monetization. Nothing comforts a customer more than knowing you have helped to solve a similar problem already. You will get to the point where instead of you looking for customers, customers will be looking for *you*, as the power of word of mouth and networks will shift you from the constant-pursuit level to the law-of-attraction level. Not only will you attract ready customers, willing and able to pay your asking price but above all, you will attract customers who identify with your vision and connect on other levels.

Takeaways

The key to moving out of the vulnerable valley in order to monetize your idea is to have it embodied in a *product*—something that can easily be presented to the market for individuals to choose and consume. However, this cannot be done without first understanding how the market works and what your marketing messaging should include. Monetizing creativity involves creating connections with people and solving their problems in your unique way. Even if you were to have management representation, you still need to understand your niche.

Your creativity has value, value that people will gladly pay for. Setting yourself apart and creating a competitive advantage boosts your ability to monetize your creativity. And the best competitive advantage you can have is YOU! Your unique combination of skills, talent, experience, and creativity may be imitated but can never be duplicated.

NOTES

CHAPTER 9

Protecting It!
Create It, Own It, Keep It.

"Creativity is an energy. It's a precious energy, and it's something to be protected. A lot of people take for granted that they're a creative person, but I know from experience, feeling it in myself, it is a magic; it is an energy. And it can't be taken for granted."
– Ava DuVernay

"Alvin! Aaaaallllvin!"

"Yes, Dave?"

If you are familiar with *Alvin & The Chipmunks*, you will recognize the above dialogue. *The Chipmunks* were one of the cartoons widely admired by children the world over for decades. Ross Bagdasarian, Sr. created *The Chipmunks* in 1958 when he used his tape recorder to speed up his voice. The series is all about three animated rodents representing record label executives and being managed by their human adoptive father.

Bagdasarian, Sr. created hits with his voicing of *The Chipmunks*. He ensured that not only the rights to *The Chipmunks* remained in the family but also the rights to all the master recordings, animations, and even characters. He was the *first* songwriter to own not just the publishing rights but also the master recordings.

However, his death in 1972 saw a slow-down in *The Chipmunks'* output. Ross Bagdasarian, Jr. had little interest in the family business. His father had urged him to go to law school, and it was only later that Bagdasarian, Jr. realized that his father wasn't urging him

129

to go to law school to practice law but to understand how to protect the creative rights of *The Chipmunks* and keep them in the family. Bagdasarian, Jr. later revived *The Chipmunks* with his wife, Janice Karman. Together they took *The Chipmunks* brand to new heights and significantly increased the value of the brand.

In 1985, as they negotiated to air their first season on NBC, they would often have to use their own money, not receiving the full benefit that the brand had to offer. They received only $200,000 (equivalent to $467,000 in 2019) for the first season of *Alvin & The Chipmunks,* which was not enough to cover all the costs to produce and air the episodes.

As *The Chipmunks* were making a comeback, CBS Viacom wanted to run Bagdasarian, Sr.'s old shows against the current NBC shows. In an attempt to not have Viacom run the old episodes and thus dilute the value of the current shows, Bagdasarian, Jr. and Janice were willing to offer the syndication rights to Viacom, but fortunately Viacom refused. (A broadcast syndication is a license to broadcast programs through radio, television, and other platforms without having to go through a broadcast network.)

They later sold the syndication rights for $25 million! (Equivalent to $58 million in 2019.)

In crafting your creativity, you need to be aware that your creative idea may be reproduced, redistributed, or used without your permission or consent *if* you don't take the necessary steps and precautions to protect it. What's even worse is when your idea is stolen outright and used to generate money for someone else with *no* benefits accruing to you. In my courses and talks, I always include information about Intellectual Property and I always advocate for creative work to be protected.

This is why I didn't ask you to share your crazy idea during the blow-the-lid-off activity. I simply wanted you to make a declaration—and to show us your art skills, of course!

Intellectual Property (IP)

Intellectual Property (IP) refers to creations of the mind: Inventions, literary and artistic works, and symbols, names, and images used in commerce. Along with this property are rights of creation and protection, just as with other property. *Intellectual Property Rights* are outlined in Article 27 of the Universal Declaration of Human Rights and also protected in law by individual countries. These rights ensure that you are duly rewarded for your creativity.

Your first assignment is to find out if your country has Intellectual Property laws and how they function. The United Nations developed WIPO (World Intellectual Property Organization) in 1970 through the WIPO Convention signed in Stockholm in 1967.

There are different aspects to IP, so you need to identify which one suits your particular creative case.

Patent: This is an exclusive right to an invention and is usually common in scientific circles. This invention, however, must be something new and groundbreaking, never before seen or used. A patent lasts for 20 years, after which it goes into the public domain, but it can be renewed by making modifications. The patent owner is the one who will decide who can and cannot use the invention and if permission is given, the monetary rewards must accrue back to the original creator.

Trademark: A trademark is a uniquely recognizable sign or symbol that represents a particular good or service. This IP protection is used to protect brand logos, which are a combination of words, letters, and/or numbers. It can even include 3-D symbols and drawings. Trademarking is extremely useful to protect yourself from counterfeits and copycat competitors leveraging your creative work. A trademark lasts for 10 years. Trademarks (as well as patents) are territorial and only provide protection in the country of registration. However, WIPO also administers an international application registration system.

Industrial Design: This refers to the aesthetic appeal of an article. It concerns the artistic design of a product or packaging. Industrial design applications range from mobile phones to luxury items to handicrafts to bottles. Technical features are not covered here but they can be covered under a patent. Industrial Design lasts for 10 years with renewable options.

Copyright: [33]This grants authors, artists, and other creators protection for their literary and artistic creations. Works covered by copyright include but are not limited to: Novels, poems, plays, reference works, newspapers, advertisements, computer programs, databases, films, musical compositions, choreography, paintings, drawings, photographs, sculpture, architecture, maps, and technical drawings. This protection grants the authors of the work the right to authorize and prohibit any reproduction, distribution, or transition in any form or by any means. The work produced here must be in a permanent form of expression and not just an idea. A copyright usually lasts up to 70 years post the death of the author.

The above is just an introduction to IP so as to raise awareness when one is dealing with creative work. Always seek advice from an IP lawyer or relevant expert regarding your situation and your best course of action. Do not take these matters lightly; this is your life's work and you deserve to be compensated whenever your idea is used commercially. It is also important that you be aware of instances when you use the work of others and who owns the rights to such work, e.g., if you are a photographer and you cover an event, do you own the rights to commercially use those images?

I want to give you some MAMI (Minor Adjustments => Major Improvements) tips that can help you in your journey to imple-

---

[33] World Intellectual Property Organization, "What Is Intellectual Property," WIPO Publication, No. 450(E).

mentation and boost your IP skills with your creative work from the imagination stage to the commercial level.

Keep it to yourself. Be careful that a random conversation does not lead you to "spilling the beans" regarding your new idea *before* it is ready to be released. As much as your idea may be revolutionary, it is still in the infancy stage if it is not yet embodied into a product that can be protected. There are times when you may need to divulge your new idea at the infancy stage, but ensure you do it in a safe environment, as discussed further below.

Nondisclosure agreements (NDAs). When the need does arise for you to share your creative idea with someone, either for guidance or funding, then ensure that prior to sharing anything you get an NDA drafted and signed between both parties. This confidentiality agreement ensures that if the party with whom you intend to share your idea turns around and uses it, or inadvertently shares it with someone who goes ahead and uses it without your permission, then you will have legal redress. Because this is a legally binding document, you will want a lawyer, and preferably an IP lawyer, to draft this for you. Avoid using random templates from the internet as they may not fully cover you.

Documentation. You will need to learn how to document the journey of your creative idea: Who you spoke to, when you spoke to them, what were the contents of the discussion, and was this in person or over the internet. This builds a paper trail that tells the story of your journey and can be used in your defense should the need arise. By sharing your ideas with others, you might get suggestions for improvements from them, and you want to avoid that person later on claiming that you stole their idea. Try as much as possible not to share your idea over the internet or through email, even if it is an attachment. Insist on face-to-face meetings (where applicable) in which the other party can be given a hard copy to read during the meeting and return it to you after the meeting.

Research. Prior to deciding to work with someone, or with an organization, on your idea, ensure you do as much research as possible regarding the nature of their work and who they have worked with before. Check their track record and check for complaints in order to get a feel for their character. Don't be in too much of a hurry to get going and get your idea into the marketplace; take your time and do the necessary due diligence. You might find that they have a similar plan but want to connect with you to get ideas to improve their own idea. Try to ensure that you use referrals for connections so you at least have a reference point.

Contracts. Once you decide to begin working with someone, either as a partner, collaborator, or even hiring employees, ensure that you have contracts that both parties agree to and sign prior to the work commencing. A noncompete clause or separate contract should be used at this point. A contract is simply a meeting of minds and reflects the intentions of both parties. Don't rely on trust or word of mouth; if it's not written, then it essentially didn't happen or wasn't agreed to.

Apart from the legal and nonlegal protection mechanisms you can use to protect your creativity, you need to also protect and manage your emotions.

EI (Emotional Intelligence)

Emotional Intelligence, or emotional quotient (EQ), is defined as an individual's ability to identify, evaluate, control, and express their emotions. It is being aware of your emotions and the emotions of others, and leveraging your emotions to be more effective. The creative journey and the journey of self-discovery can equally be a journey filled with emotions: Emotions of happiness and excitement when you see your creativity come to life, and also emotions of sadness and disappointment when your creative juices and ideas just don't seem to be flowing or to be accepted by others. Understanding how emotions fit into your creative journey and how to ensure that you protect that creative energy is vital to the success of your journey.

Firstly, emotions are not necessarily good or bad; they are data points signaling what's going on with you. Both "good" and "bad" emotions are a reality of life and they both make life worth living. There are moments for laughter and happiness and there are moments for sadness and crying. Often, we are socialized to display only our "good" emotions and to hide our "bad" emotions. Along the creative journey, you will experience both *passion fatigue* and *decision fatigue*, so having the discipline and consistency to deal with these feelings is a key step to continued success.

Secondly, understanding the feedback your emotions are giving you, and using it to make informed decisions, is key in dealing with your emotions over the course of your creative journey. You need to be able to identify which emotions need to be increased, decreased, or prolonged, and it's not as easy as saying increase the good ones and decrease the bad ones. Both sets of emotions, when properly managed, can contribute positively to the expression of your creative gene.

Thirdly, you can experience more than one emotion at the same time, and also experience both positive and negative emotions simultaneously. Emotional ambivalence is a particularly complex emotion, characterized by tension and conflict, that is felt when someone experiences both positive and negative emotions simultaneously (Lori Friedman). During my earlier experiences of public speaking, I would get on stage and feel quite nervous but very excited at the same time. Nervous because I would constantly be thinking about what would happen if I made a mistake; excited because I was given an opportunity where people wanted to hear what I had to say.

American psychologist Daniel Goleman states that there are five key elements to Emotional Intelligence:

Self-awareness: This means that you need to be aware of and receptive to your situation and to stay emotionally in tune with your surroundings and what your dominant emotions are at different times. It also means accepting what you are good at as well as the areas that you struggle with.

Self-regulation: This means being able to control your emotions and not allowing them to run wild. You move to a point where you don't just react to your emotions; instead, you think and then you respond. Also, don't be quick to blame others if you aren't in control; instead, take control by pausing or taking deep breaths.

Motivation: This means choosing to be optimistic and to be real with yourself and your goals, choosing to focus more on your why than on your how, and letting your passion and enthusiasm drive you.

Empathy: This means taking the time to notice and be aware of the emotions of others so you can create better relationships.

Social skills: This means being friendly with a purpose (as Goleman puts it), leveraging your friendliness to communicate effectively, to appreciate and applaud others for their good work, and to resolve conflicts diplomatically.

Emotional Intelligence Promotes Creativity

Sergio Agnoli of The Marconi Institute for Creativity in Italy led a research project seeking to answer the question, "Why are some individuals able to generate outstanding creative products despite repeated, frustrating failures?" The study revealed the answer to be "how people experience and regulate their emotions."

The common narrative is that creativity and imagination are accompanied by emotional problems. However, the study revealed that higher levels of creativity are linked to self-awareness, which facilitates navigating the ups and downs of the creative journey.

Being emotionally intelligent allows you to treat irrelevant stimuli (such as a failure message from others) as potentially helpful and to incorporate it into your thinking through cognitive integration, thus modulating the effects of the feelings and using them to fuel you to carry on. However, if the thought or sign of failure derails you, this will be much more difficult, as you are not able to use it as a stepping stone but instead see it as irritating and frustrating. The study offers Vincent van Gogh as an example of being "able to extract energy from deep frustration to produce some of the most beautiful works of art our world has known."

The resounding message is that being emotionally intelligent or having a high EQ leads to more success both personally and professionally, but more importantly, it increases your creativity.

Takeaways

Your creativity is unique and valuable. It must, therefore, be protected and guarded. Intellectual Property (IP) law provides creators of work and imagination protection from unauthorized use of their work. IP law provides a systematic avenue for how your creativity may be shared, ensuring that you receive due recognition and reward for your work. Protection must be taken on as a personal responsibility under professional guidance.

Creativity is also your energy, and it requires protection from attacks of fatigue and lack of emotional awareness and control. There is a very emotive nature to creativity which cannot be avoided but can be leveraged. Emotional Intelligence is a skill that can be learned, and it can be used to positively impact the creative process by giving you that staying power in your creative journey to solve problems and produce artistic work. Your creativity will blossom and you will have the inner satisfaction and external validation that comes when you have created something of value.

Emotional Intelligence, or emotional quotient **(EQ)**, is defined as an individual's ability to identify, evaluate, control, and express emotions.

NOTES

_____

_____

_____

_____

_____

_____

_____

_____

_____

_____

_____

_____

_____

_____

_____

_____

CHAPTER 10

In Conclusion
Live Your Legacy

"There are two great days in a person's life – the day we are born and the day we discover why."
– **William Barclay**

Your creative path is only beginning.

The discovery of your creative gene and blowing the lid off can be a life-defining occurrence. Creativity will not be just an abstract concept but a crucial component of your life and your mission. These are compelling reasons why we should care about, and be concerned about, not just our own creativity but the creativity of others. Living a crazy, creative life empowers you to be a great problem solver in all aspects of your life.

I hope you are now more aware that you may also be (unknowingly) suppressing someone's creative gene. As a parent, your child should be constantly nurturing their creativity, even without your full understanding as a prerequisite. One child may show stronger creative tendencies than another. The best route to follow here is that of facilitating both children to achieve excellence in the achievement of their goals according to their unique learning abilities. Remember that creativity often goes against the grain and sees beyond what is obvious, thus care should be taken to be understanding and supportive.

As an individual, give yourself time and room to grow your creativity, as your brain may initially resist original thinking by applying cognitive filters and biases before any thought or idea is fully developed or produced. Be true to those crazy ideas you wrote down earlier in the book. Don't give up on them, don't let them go, and hold them close to you until it's time to let them out into the world. But don't wait until perfection is attained to let them out.

Benefits of creative living

As teachers and guardians, let us teach our children to be tactful in unleashing their creativity. Help them identify their unique gifts, talents, and imagination to solve problems. We never want to suppress their creative gene; we want them to know how and when to switch it off to avoid being offensive with it.

Creative living improves self-confidence and self-awareness, allowing you to unapologetically live your mission, not being worried about standing out or not fitting in, and liberating yourself from the fear of being wrong. I am "me" no matter where I am. What is your identity apart from your profession and other societal labels? Just to remind you, mine are Champion of creativity, Ambassador of wellness, and Pursuer of excellence. Share with me yours online using the hashtag #BlowTheLidOff.

Have the self-confidence to go for what you believe is possible, just as President Barack Obama said, "Yes we can." Yes, a man of black African heritage can rise to be the President of The United States of America.

That light bulb moment that you have is your perfect opportunity to let your light shine and to illuminate new possibilities.

The nonlinear, creative approach to living assists you in being able to handle uncertainty, as situations can be viewed and approached from different angles, unlocking aspects that may not have been possible previously.

"Intelligence is an important initial requirement for creativity in all domains; it is virtually impossible to be intentionally creative without some level of intellectual ability. In a similar way, divergent thinking could be an initial requirement for creativity in all domains. That is, without the ability to view an idea from different angles, it is difficult, if not impossible, to produce creative ideas."[34]

Therefore, being open to change is core to continued success. "Without change there is no innovation, creativity, or incentive for improvement. Those who initiate change will have a better opportunity to manage the change that is inevitable." – **William Pollard**

Creativity for now and the future

The rate of change in today's world is exponential. This provides a lucrative environment for creativity. We can even see creativity as a catalyst for this rapid rate of change. Therefore, the comfort zone must constantly change if one is to reap the benefits at each stage of change. As a creative, you will notice your difficulty with sticking to one place (physically, energetically, or mentally). You will continually explore new challenges, and this desire for constant change can often be misinterpreted. Personally, I have a passion for creating sustainable structures out of chaos, but once the structures are in place, I desire a new assignment.

"I love creating new things. It's difficult to be creative once a restaurant's open. People want the same dishes. For me, creativity is in opening a new place and starting a new menu." – **Jean-Georges Vongerichten**

Creativity is being original in problem solving and looking beyond the now. Promoting creativity is to promote the growth and development of humanity. Creativity is not only expressed

---

[34] Kim, K.H. "Meta-analyses of the relationship of creative achievement to both IQ and divergent thinking test scores," *The Journal of Creative Behavior*, **42**(2), (2008): 106– 130.

through a profession—it is a lifestyle. As a qualified accountant, I resist the urge to be rigid and I ensure that my creativity is expressed. After all, the double entry accounting system we use today was developed through creativity. The debate is ongoing as to who exactly invented the system and where, but what is known is that a book about it was produced in 1494 by an Italian mathematician named Fra Luca Pacioli and his close friend Leonardo da Vinci. They explored how accounting could be more efficient and organized so as to produce financial statements. The two leveraged each other's strengths with Pacioli writing the text and da Vinci creatively illustrating it to support the text explanation. This double entry system propelled capitalism!

These were some of the mad men of yesterday who allowed us to act with such great clarity today. Karl Weierstrass, the father of modern analysis, once wrote, "A mathematician that is not something of a poet will never be a true mathematician."

Share your creativity and encourage those around you to pursue their crazy ideas and take part in creative engagement with others. We need leaders of today who will not be afraid to blow the lid off so they can think, explore, and invent.

Participating in creativity unlocks knowledge about yourself, others, and the world around you providing an immense benefit even to those who do not consider themselves creative.[35] I want you to join this movement so that we can change the world through our creative ideas. Creativity requires a team—a team of like-minded people to bounce ideas around and to make the world a better place.

"True leaders don't invest in buildings. Jesus never built a building. They invest in people. Why? Because success without a successor is fail-

---

[35] Silvia, Paul & Beaty, Roger & Nusbaum, Emily & Eddington, Kari & Levin-Aspenson, Holly & Kwapil, Thomas. (2014). "Everyday Creativity in Daily Life: An Experience-Sampling Study of 'Little c' Creativity." Psychology of Aesthetics Creativity and the Arts. 8. 10.1037/a0035722.

*ure. So your legacy should not be in buildings, programs, or projects; your legacy must be in people." – **Myles Munroe**

Employers and corporate institutions need to promote and encourage their employees to be more creative. "Creativity is the single most in-demand skill for companies to develop in their employees."[36] Creativity is the currency of the future. When employees are more creative, they not only improve performance and productivity, they also help companies to grow even more through deeper connections with customers and consumers. Offices need to facilitate creative expression both physically and in operations. Employees should never be penalized for being creative. The Post-it Notes that we all love using were invented by an employee of 3M. It is notable (pun intended) that 3M allowed employees 15 percent of their time to pursue a creative passion not necessarily related to their day-to-day work.

Nonetheless, creativity must be *expressed* for it to have an impact. There is no certificate or qualification to certify that you are creative. You just have to experience it, try it, and fail at it until you understand and incorporate it fully. The creative journey begins with ideas and thoughts in one's mind at the mini-c level and grows to having global impact at the Big-C level.

You can continue taking steps in your own creative journey by posting to social media with the hashtag #BlowTheLidOff and sign up for updates on my website.

The Connecting power of creativity

Creativity is about connections. Connecting your inner imagination with your environment, connecting your right and left brain, connecting your ideas with people, and connecting your creative genius to problems and to the people who face those problems.

---

[36] LinkedIn Learning's 3rd Annual Workplace Learning Report, 2019.

Your creativity has value and especially when you express it in solving problems. Monetizing creativity must be done within the guidelines of trade. Buying and selling rules are guidelines. The value of creativity can only be assessed by the persons whose problems your creative idea is solving. When they do, financial and other rewards will flow back to you. The essence here is that creativity must be crafted; it must be polished.

Also, a creative idea has commercial viability and thus runs the risk of attracting copycats. Creativity can be used to generate a competitive advantage in our rapidly expanding global economy. Protecting your creative idea starts and ends with you but there are tools available to support you. Some tools are of a legal nature and must be used under the guidance of a legal professional, such as an IP lawyer. Use the tips and information in this book as a starting point and not a conclusive solution to the issue of protection.

Care should be taken in understanding the emotive nature of creativity. Emotional Intelligence or EQ is a skill and a tool that, when used correctly, can not only increase creativity but also improve its effectiveness. EQ impacts your entire being and helps you not only to navigate the choppy emotional waters of the creative journey but also to position yourself to get more out of life through your relationships.

Developing your creativity will take time. How long, you may ask? What's the average time? These questions are not relevant here, as they are generic in nature. More so, wanting to know how long it will take has the effect of programming your mind to believe that creativity is a destination to arrive at. But it's not; you are already creative; you were born with creativity. Knowing what the signs and evidence of your creativity are, is a much better avenue to pursue. Be patient with yourself. Sometimes the *process* of creating is more significant than the finished piece of work

(Pursuit of Happiness, n.d.).[37] Just keep moving forward and let your light shine.

Prioritize and nurture your creativity and be in tune with your imagination. Try something new, do something for the experience of it. Sign up for an art class or a pottery class. Learn a new (or another) instrument; learn a foreign language. Try doodling and see what comes out of it and where your mind takes you. Redesign your space to make it more conducive for creative thinking. Join our community and let us know where you would like to get support or give support.

✌

You've now read about how to *Blow the Lid Off* and craft your creativity, so go ahead and get started if you haven't already. Start where you are: As a student, as an employee, as a parent, as a retiree. Whatever stage of life you are at right now, just start and let your creative gene reveal its message. Create for the sake of creating; don't focus so much on the finished product and just enjoy the process. Learn and develop your creativity like a child learning a new language. Focus more on questions, not answers, and let this lead you to a level of creative fulfilment.

*"The most important relationship we can all have is the one we have with ourself; the most important journey you can take is one of self-discovery. To know yourself, you must spend time with yourself, you must not be afraid to be alone. Knowing yourself is the beginning of all wisdom." – **Aristotle***

From the soil of ordinary spring trees of creativity and innovation through careful reflection.

Creativity—you've got it! Use it!

---

[37] Csikszentmihalyi, Mihaly (1990). Flow: The Psychology of Optimal Experience. New York, NY: Harper and Row.

Your creative literacy and ability is not defined by your professional or educational persuasion. Remove the stereotypical biases based on your area of expertise. Know that as a qualified accountant, I understand how difficult this can be, and that is why I wrote this book—to encourage you. Creativity is one of the biggest differentiators in our world. Using it to let your light shine can lead you to live a more fulfilling life. [38]Even people who do not consider themselves creative, experience creative moments. Indeed, those in traditionally noncreative professions experience little-c creative acts nearly one-fifth of the time, as recorded by Silvia.[39] These smaller bursts of creativity were linked significantly to positive emotions, openness to experience, and conscientiousness, all of which can help one's pursuit of life goals and personal fulfilment.

Adopt my ABC of creativity—*Always Be Creative.*

Creativity in Sports

In Search of Greatness is a sports documentary, a cinematic journey into the secrets of genius through the eyes of the greatest athletes of all time. Director Gabe Polsky reveals to us that the one thing the interviewed athletes refused to compromise on was *their creative vision and values.* Athletes interviewed included Wayne Gretzky, Pelé, and Jerry Rice, and it also features Muhammad Ali, Serena Williams, Michael Jordan, and others. Polsky's motivation to do the documentary was fueled by his desire to achieve excellence and look into all the systems that can stifle creativity. The athletes revealed that unstructured time and play (playing in the backyard, making your own ball with available materials, etc.),

---

[38] Helfand, M., Kaufman, J. C., & Beghetto, R. A. (2017). "The Four C Model of Creativity: Culture and Context." In V. P. Glăveanu (Ed.), *Palgrave handbook of creativity and culture research* (pp. 15-360). New York: Palgrave.

[39] Silvia, Paul & Beaty, Roger & Nusbaum, Emily & Eddington, Kari & Levin-Aspenson, Holly & Kwapil, Thomas. (2014). "Everyday Creativity in Daily Life: An Experience-Sampling Study of 'Little c' Creativity." *Psychology of Aesthetics Creativity and the Arts.* 8. 10.1037/a0035722.

and *not* endless training and drills, is what helped foster their creativity and put them on the path to greatness.

Pelé said that the best athlete was Garrincha. He had one knee in and one knee out. This was considered a physical impossibility, but it led him to develop new dribbling skills that changed the game of soccer. Pelé himself broke away from the widely practiced strategy of all-game defense, flipping the strategy to one of aggression and scoring a record-breaking number of goals. This often caused clashes and confrontations with his coaching team, but he had the courage to just blow the lid off and not be afraid to let his personal light shine. As it turned out, his light shone both on and off the field as he broke down racial barriers in the social community.

Heavyweight boxer Rocky Marciano was much shorter and lighter than his opponents and he had a short reach. This meant he had to develop a new boxing technique by moving in closer to his opponents.

Wayne Gretzky became the first player to play behind the net. His creativity was sparked by his sense of survival. Using the net as a shield was a competitive advantage as no one else knew how to play from such a position.

"His Airness," Michael Jordan, redefined "hang time" and dominated in the post that was unusual for a shooting guard, amongst other feats.

Yes, creativity definitely helps in sports. The documentary, however, is not all about sports, as others such as The Beatles, Mozart, and Einstein were also studied revealing similar tendencies to those of the athletes.

The take-home message here is that creativity "resonates beyond the world of sport to the realms of self-expression, psychology, philosophy, and human nature."[40]

---

[40] In Search of Greatness. Dir. Gabe Polsky. Gravitas Ventures, 2018.

Phil Knight, the founder of the sporting and apparel company Nike, outlines the start of his entrepreneurial journey in his memoir, *Shoe Dog*. He started the company with "a crazy idea"—importing Japanese running shoes into the US. This stemmed from his MBA course requirements while at Stanford Graduate School of Business, and he travelled the world to spark his imagination and personal inspiration. His first shipment took about a year to arrive, and in that time (thanks to advice from his father), he acquired his CPA qualifications and worked as an accountant. Once the shipment arrived, he went full time into selling shoes. He would, however, go back into accounting working as an auditor at Price Waterhouse and even taught accounting at Portland State University in order to have a fallback plan. He used this opportunity to keep his dream and crazy idea alive by studying companies and "learning how they survived, or didn't." During this time, his company (Blue Ribbon) continued to operate.

When Nike was officially incorporated (and now making their own shoes, and later sporting apparel) it consisted mainly of accountants and lawyers. Knight's thoughts were that accountants "…had proved they could master a difficult subject and pass a big test." Knight, being an accountant himself, refused to believe that accountants couldn't be creative or innovative. In his personal search for greatness, he would often quote General McArthur:

"Don't tell people how to do things; tell them what to do and let them surprise you with their results." He favored a leadership style over a managerial style, as he did not want to suppress the creativity of others. Reflecting back on this unusual recruitment strategy, he said, "My management style wouldn't have worked for people who wanted to be guided every step, but this group found it liberating, empowering."

What a way to blow the lid off! Just do it.

❧

I want to close this book by paying tribute to my maternal grandmother, Priscilla Ingasiani Abwao. Guku (the Maragoli name for grandmother) had a profound impact on my creativity and imagination from an early age, both through her instruction and how she lived her life. Guku lived beyond her time, refusing to allow the limitations of any situation to stop her. Every challenge was an opportunity for her creativity to be utilized to overcome it. Her creativity was also expressed through her passion to fight for women's rights, and she was a trailblazer with an indomitable spirit.

Mrs. Abwao's fight for gender equality, coupled with her unique sense of creativity, led her to be known throughout the country. In 1961, she was nominated and appointed by the governor of Kenya to the LegCo (Legislative Council) making her the first African woman in the all-male parliament in Kenya. She would later that year join the team that travelled to London to participate in the Lancaster Constitutional Talks. These talks were a key component in the process of Kenya drafting a constitution, then being granted self-rule and eventually achieving independence from colonial rule. Mrs. Abwao would later participate in and advocate for the release of Kenya's founding father, Mzee (Mr.) Jomo Kenyatta.

I was quite unsettled as a child, and frankly I did strange things just for attention. One day, when I was eight years old, she pulled me into her office and advised me to consider others during my times of outburst. She then began to show me how the business of running a farm worked—something she knew I would most certainly be interested in…and then not have time for anything else. Her office was well organized and full of books and ledgers, and I was amazed at the level of professionalism and attention to detail she had when it came to her work. As grandchildren, we had never been allowed to go into the office without her permission.

Now she showed me how each of her 100 cows were producing and their daily expected output, thus teaching me about asset utilization. She took me through the planted vegetables, when they were likely to be harvested, and the expected harvest quantity.

Then it came to money matters, and here we delved deeply. The area that caught my eye was the payroll. She showed me the salary and wage amounts of each worker, and I had the opportunity to participate in the experience from start to end. We sat down and she showed me how the workers' pay was calculated and which ledger book needed to be used. Once the overall total was known, we then had to calculate the cash breakdown. I had to label and put the cash in the labeled envelopes ready for distribution to the workers.

This is perhaps why today I have money talks with my own children from an early age. One day while washing dishes, my five-year-old daughter wanted to count her money from her money box. Somehow the discussion shifted towards taxation and I took the opportunity to give her a first lesson in taxes and tax planning. It was so smooth and natural. The next topic I want to discuss with her is the time value of money.

Priscilla Abwao, I salute you as my creative hero. May your soul rest in peace.

Creativity must be nurtured and given an opportunity to thrive so it can have an impact and be developed to solve problems. Let's give ourselves a chance—every one of us—to live a crazy, creative life!

THE END

Endnotes

[1] Cropley, A.J. (2014). "Neglect of creativity in education: A moral issue." In S. Moran, D.H. Cropley & J.C. Kaufman (Eds.), The ethics of creativity (pp. 250–264). New York: Palgrave Macmillan.

[2] Tan, O.S. (2015). "Flourishing creativity: Education in an age of wonder." Asia Pacific Education Review, 16, 161–166. https://doi.org/10.1007/s12564-015-9377-6.

[3] United Nations. General Assembly. 71/284-World Creativity and Innovation Day. April 27, 2017.

[4] United Nations Conference on Trade and Development. Creative Economic Outlook Report.

[5] Ernest & Young, "Cultural Times, The first global map of cultural and creative industries," December 2015.

[6] Georgetown University, "Recovery: Job Growth and Education Requirements Through 2020," 2014.

[7] ACCA, "Drivers of change and future skills," June 2016.

[8] Boden, J. E., & Boden, G. M. (1969). "The other side of the brain III: The corpus callosum and creativity." Bulletin of the Los Angeles Neurological Society, 34, 191-203.

[9] Sternberg, R. J., & Lubart, T. I. (1999). "The concept of creativity: Prospects and paradigms." In R. J. Sternberg (Ed.), Handbook of creativity (pp. 3-15). Cambridge: Cambridge University Press.

[10] Arne Dietrich, "The cognitive neuroscience of creativity," *Psychonomic Bulletin & Review*, 11 (6), 1011, 2004.

[11] Helfand, M., Kaufman, J. C., & Beghetto, R. A. (2017). "The Four C Model of Creativity: Culture and Context." In V. P. Glăveanu (Ed.), Palgrave handbook of creativity and culture research (pp. 15-360). New York: Palgrave.

[12] Helfand, M., Kaufman, J. C., & Beghetto, R. A. (2017). "The Four C Model of Creativity: Culture and Context." In V. P. Glăveanu (Ed.), Palgrave handbook of creativity and culture research (p. 19). New York: Palgrave.

[13] Cowan N. "Attention and memory: An integrated framework." New York, NY, US: Oxford University Press; 1995.

[14] Posner MI, Dehaene S. "Attentional networks." Trends Neurosci. 1994 Feb;17(2):75–79.

[15] Helfand, M., Kaufman, J. C., & Beghetto, R. A. (2017). "The Four C Model of Creativity: Culture and Context." In V. P. Glăveanu (Ed.), *Palgrave handbook of creativity and culture research* (pp. 15-360). New York: Palgrave.

[16] Maslow, Abraham. *Motivation and Personality.* New York: Harper & Brothers, 1954.

[17] Runco, M. A. Problem finding, problem solving, and creativity. California: Greenwood Publishing Group, 1994.

[18] Vandenberg, B, "Problem-solving and creativity," In K.H. Rubin (Ed.), New Directions for Child Development: Children's Play. San Fransisco: Jossey-Bass, 1980.

[19] Striker, Susan. Young at Art: Teaching Toddlers Self-Expression, Problem-Solving Skills, and an Appreciation for Art. New York: Holt, Henry & Company, Inc., 2001.

[20] "Test Anxiety," American Test Anxieties Association, http://amtaa.org.

[21] Sarason, S.B., Davidson, K.S., Lighthall, F.F. et al. Anxiety in elementary school children. New York: Wiley, 1960.

[22] Wikipedia contributors, "J. P. Guilford," Wikipedia, *The Free Encyclopedia*, https://en.wikipedia.org/w/index.php?title=J._P._Guilford&oldid=914820318 (accessed October 24, 2019).

ENDNOTES

[23]United Nations Development Programme, "Human Development Index (HDI)," *Human Development Reports*, 2017.

[24] The Editors of Encyclopaedia Britannica, "Cubism," *Encyclopaedia Britannica, Inc.*, June 20, 2019. https://www.britannica.com/art/Cubism.

[25]Silvia, Paul & Beaty, Roger & Nusbaum, Emily & Eddington, Kari & Levin-Aspenson, Holly & Kwapil, Thomas. (2014). "Everyday Creativity in Daily Life: An Experience-Sampling Study of 'Little c' Creativity." Psychology of Aesthetics Creativity and the Arts. 8. 10.1037/a0035722.

[26] Newberry, Tommy. Success Is Not an Accident: Change Your Choices; Change Your Life. Illinois: Tyndale House Publishers, 2007.

[27] Lamore, Rex & Root-Bernstein, Robert & Root-Bernstein, Michele & Schweitzer, John & Lawton, James & Roraback, Eileen & Peruski, Amber & VanDyke, Megan & Fernandez, Laleah. (2013). "Arts and Crafts Critical to Economic Innovation." Economic Development Quarterly. 27. 221-229. 10.1177/0891242413486186.

[28] Stephen M. Kosslyn, Ph.D. and G. Wayne Miller, "The Theory of Cognitive Modes," Psychology Today: October 2015.

[29] Klaus D. Hoppe & Neville L. Kyle, "Dual brain, creativity, and health," Creativity Research Journal, 3:2, (1990) 150-157, DOI: 10.1080/10400419009534348.

[30] Leung, A. K., Maddux, W. W., Galinksy, A. D., & Chiu, C.-Y. (2008). "Multicultural experience enhances creativity." American Psychologist, 63(3), 169–181. DOI:10.1037/0003-066X.63.3.169.

[31] Leung, A. K., & Chiu, C.-Y. (2010). "Multicultural experience, idea receptiveness, and creativity." Journal of Cross-Cultural Psychology, 41, 723–741. DOI:10.1177/0022022110361707.

[32] Simonton, D. K. (2000). "Creativity: Cognitive, personal, developmental, and social aspects." American Psychologist, 55, 151–158. doi:10.1037/ 0003-066X.55.1.151.

[33] World Intellectual Property Organization, "What Is Intellectual Property," WIPO Publication, No. 450(E).

[34] Kim, K.H. "Meta-analyses of the relationship of creative achievement to both IQ and divergent thinking test scores," *The Journal of Creative Behavior*, 42(2), (2008): 106– 130.

[35] Silvia, Paul & Beaty, Roger & Nusbaum, Emily & Eddington, Kari & Levin-Aspenson, Holly & Kwapil, Thomas. (2014). "Everyday Creativity in Daily Life: An Experience-Sampling Study of 'Little c' Creativity." Psychology of Aesthetics Creativity and the Arts. 8. 10.1037/a0035722.

[36] LinkedIn Learning's 3rd Annual Workplace Learning Report, 2019.

[37] Csikszentmihalyi, Mihaly (1990). Flow: The Psychology of Optimal Experience. New York, NY: Harper and Row.

[38] Helfand, M., Kaufman, J. C., & Beghetto, R. A. (2017). "The Four C Model of Creativity: Culture and Context." In V. P. Glăveanu (Ed.), *Palgrave handbook of creativity and culture research* (pp. 15-360). New York: Palgrave.

[39] Silvia, Paul & Beaty, Roger & Nusbaum, Emily & Eddington, Kari & Levin-Aspenson, Holly & Kwapil, Thomas. (2014). "Everyday Creativity in Daily Life: An Experience-Sampling Study of 'Little c' Creativity." *Psychology of Aesthetics Creativity and the Arts*. 8. 10.1037/a0035722.

[40] In Search of Greatness. Dir. Gabe Polsky. Gravitas Ventures, 2018.